Rev. Thomas J. Shelley

# NEW

## The History of

## the Archdiocese of

# YORK

# CONTENTS

# NEW
The History of
the Archdiocese of
# YORK

preface

Preface by John Cardinal O'Connor
Archbishop of New York,

As we enter the Jubilee Year, which marks the end of the second millenium of the Christian era and the beginning of the third, it is appropriate to reflect on the struggles and achievements of the past in light of our own lives and times. We also look to the future to see what kind of people we want to be, as we try to live out our Catholic faith in a changing world.

In the light of this, it is appropriate that we have before us this combined History of the Archdiocese of New York. Here, we have the record of how the Church in New York shaped the history of New York City and of the United States as well. In part, it is a record of how Catholics struggled for their faith, endured hardships and great sacrifices in spreading the faith to other parts of the country. It is a story of commitment and heroism, victory and tragedy, a true participation in the sufferings of Christ. At the same time, it is the story of ordinary people doing extraordinary things as they help to build up the Kingdom of God here in the Archdiocese of New York. That story comes vividly to life in the very fine writing of Father Thomas Shelley, and in the wonderful photographs and illustrations which fill the book.

As I wrote in the preface to the first volume of this History, the obstacles faced by the men and women who came before us might seem very different from the obstacles we face today, but the challenge is the same: how do we bring the Good News to a people who might not always want to hear what we have to say? That challenge will accompany us into the New Millenium and, I am certain until the end of time. It is my belief that this History of the Archdiocese of New York can help to inspire us to not lose courage as we do our very best in bringing the Gospel message to our world today.

May God bless you.

THERE CAN BE NO LOVE WITHOUT JUSTICE

# Introduction

## The Thirteen English Colonies

Between 1607 and 1733 an unknown number of adventuresome Englishmen and Englishwomen crossed the Atlantic in fragile sailing vessels to establish permanent settlements in the wilderness of North America. Each of the thirteen colonies was founded for a specific purpose and developed its own particular identity. Only toward the end of the colonial period, under the threat of impending revolution, did the thirteen colonies learn to work together, and together they eventually created the United States of America.

English North America was an overwhelmingly Protestant world in the colonial period and would remain so well into the era of the new American Republic. These Protestant colonists may not have been especially fervent church-goers, and they were themselves divided into rival denominations. Yet there was one common element in their religious beliefs that united them, and that was a detestation of Roman Catholicism, or, as they would have said, "Popery."

By the seventeeth century anti-Catholicism had become an essential ingredient in English nationalism, nourished by the recollection of such events as the reign of "Bloody Mary" Tudor (1553-1558), the defeat of the Spanish Armada in 1588, and the Gunpowder Plot of 1605. The English colonists arriving in Jamestown in 1607 or in Plymouth in 1620 brought with them all of the anti-Catholic prejudice of the mother country, and they celebrated Guy Fawkes Day on November 5th every year with as much enthusiasm as anyone in England. The fact that there were so few Catholics among them did little to lessen their fears of Rome, for they knew that just west of the Appalachian Mountains were the nefarious French and their savage Indian allies, constant reminders of the ubiquitous perils of Popery.

**COLONIAL AMERICA**

QUEBEC
1608

PLYMOUTH
1620

JAMESTOWN
1607

SANTA FE
1609

ST AUGUSTINE
1565

SAN JUAN PUERTO RICO
1511

ENGLISH

FRENCH

SPANISH

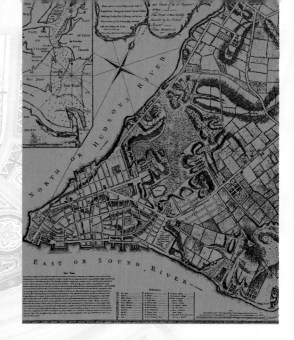

## Catholics in the English Colonies

Neither Anglican Virginia nor Puritan Massachusetts welcomed Catholic settlers. In fact, in only four of the thirteen colonies were there any Catholics at all. Along the Potomac in tidewater Virginia, the civil authorities connived at the existence of a few Catholic landowners.

Maryland, founded in 1634, was the one English colony started specifically by and for beleaguered Catholics. For the first twenty years of its existence, under the proprietorship of the Catholic Calverts, Catholics prospered in Maryland and offered religious toleration to all Christians. However, by the end of the seventeenth century, Maryland Catholics, who numbered about ten percent of the population, had lost all political power and were reduced to the private practice of their religion.

The colony where Catholics were treated best was Pennsylvania, founded in 1681 by William Penn as a place of refuge for his fellow Quakers. The Quakers were among the few Christians of that era who not only wanted religious toleration for themselves but were willing to grant it to others. The oldest Catholic church in what were the thirteen colonies is St. Joseph's Church in Philadelphia, which dates from 1733. A plaque reminds visitors that, at the time of its construction, it was the only place in the whole English-speaking world (except for the Catholic embassies in London) where it was legal to celebrate Mass.

# Catholics

## IN COLONIAL NEW YORK

New Netherlands

The only other colony with any Catholic history in the colonial period was New York, and here the Catholic presence - ephemeral as it was - dates back to the era when the Dutch controlled the Hudson River Valley. European Catholics were as unwelcome in the New Netherlands as they were in New England.

Blessed Kateri Tekakwitha, c. 1656-1680

Beginning in 1642, however, French Jesuits ventured south from Canada to evangelize the Native Americans in the Finger Lakes region and the Mohawk Valley. The French missionaries won few converts among the fiercely independent Iroquois and ended their efforts in 1709. However, they did produce one notable convert in the person of Kateri Tekakwitha, a young Indian girl who died in Canada in 1680 and was beatified in 1980. The story of these French Jesuit missionaries is one of the great sagas in North America colonial history. Their fortitude and heroism even won the admiration of Francis Parkman, the nineteenth-century Boston Brahmin historian.

Three of these North American Martyrs were put to death in upstate New York, René Goupil in 1642, and Jean Lalande and Isaac Jogues in 1646. Jogues had earlier been captured and savagely tortured by the Iroquois. After escaping from them in 1643 with the help of the Dutch, he spent a month in New Amsterdam ("the Island of Manhattes," he called it) on his way home to France. The Dutch treated him kindly, and he reported that he encountered two Catholics, a Portuguese woman and an Irishman from Virginia. Jogues received a hero's welcome on his return to France; even the Queen of France asked to see him. He could have remained there for the rest of his life, enjoying the adulation of the dévots. Instead, he chose to return to the Iroquois, who repaid his kindness by murdering him in 1646 near present-day Auriesville.

## ST. ISAAC JOGUES' DESCRIPTION OF MANHATTAN 1643

On the Island of Manhattes and in its environs there are about four or five hundred men of various sects and nations. The director general told me that eighteen different languages were spoken there. The inhabitants of the Island are scattered here and there, up and down the stream, according as the beauty or convenience of the sites invited each one to settle...

The river, very straight and flowing from north to south, is at least a league wide in front of the fort. Ships anchor in a bay on the other side of the island, and can be defended by the fort...

No exercise of religion except Calvinism is permitted there according to their laws. However, their laws are not enforced, for besides the Calvinists there are Catholics, English Puritans, Lutherans, Anabaptists (whom they call Mnistes), and many others living in the settlement.

St. Isaac Jogues, 1643, in *An Autobiography of Martyrdom: Spiritual Writings of the Jesuits in New France*, ed. François Roustang, S.J. (St. Louis, 1964), 260-261.

## ST. ISAAC JOGUES IN MANHATTAN, 1643

This good Father (Isaac Jogues) was received in Manate with great tokens of affection; the Captain had a black coat made for him. The inhabitants came to see him, showing by their looks and their words that they felt great sympathy for him...

A good lad, having met him in a retired place, fell at his feet - taking his hands to kiss them and exclaiming, "Martyr, Martyr of Jesus Christ!" He questioned him and ascertained that he was a Lutheran, whom he could not aid for want of acquaintance with his language; he was a Pole. Entering a house quite near the fort, he saw two images on the mantlepiece - one, of the blessed Virgin; the other of our Blessed Louys de Gonzage. When he betokened some satisfaction at this, the master of the house told him that his wife was a Catholic. She was a Portuguese...

An Irish Catholic, arriving at Manate from Virginia, confessed to the Father and told him that there were some of our Fathers in those regions... Finally, the Governor of the country, sending a bark of one hundred tons to Holland, sent the Father back at the beginning of the month of November (1643).

Jerome Lalement, S.J., Relation of 1647, in *The Jesuit Relations and Allied Documents*, ed. Reuben Thwaites (Cleveland, 1898), XXXI, 97-99.

## New Netherlands Becomes New York

In 1664 the New Netherlands passed into the hands of the English. The English King, Charles II, gave the new colony to his brother James, Duke of York. In 1670 James became a Catholic and four years later granted religious liberty to the inhabitants of New York.

In 1683 he took a further step and appointed as governor Thomas Dongan, Earl of Limerick, who was an Irish Catholic. In 1685 James himself succeeded to the English throne as King James II, the first Catholic sovereign since Mary Tudor. However, his reign was to be even shorter than that of "Bloody Mary." In 1688 he was toppled from the throne in a bloodless coup d'état that Whig historians celebrated as the Glorious Revolution.

In the meantime, however, in 1683, at Dongan's behest, the New York colonial assembly passed a "Charter of Liberties and Privileges" granting religious freedom to all Christians. This New York law deserves to be remembered along with the more famous Maryland Act of Religious Toleration of 1649 as an example of American Catholic commitment to the principle of religious freedom. Taking advantage of the new religious climate, three English Jesuits arrived in New York City to open a small Latin school. Father Thomas Harvey came in 1683, Father Henry Harrison in 1685, and Father Charles Gage in 1686. The first Mass was celebrated by Father Harvey on October 30, 1683, in Fort James near the site of the former U.S. Custom House. Dongan's motives in encouraging the activities of the Jesuits were political as well as religious. He wished to use them eventually in upstate New York to counteract the influence of the French Jesuits among the Indians. Indeed, one historian said of Dongan that "this Catholic governor was probably the most persistent and aggressive defender of British interests in North America."

### THE CHARTER OF LIBERTIES AND PRIVILEDGES GRANTED BY HIS ROYALL HIGHNESSE TO THE INHABITANTS OF NEW YORK AND ITS DEPENDENCYES. OCTOBER 30, 1683.

That Noe person or persons which professe faith in God by Jesus Christ Shall at any time be any wayes molested punished disquieted or called in Question for any Difference in opinion or Matter of Religious Concernment, who doe not actually disturb the Civil peace of the province, but that all and every such person or persons may from time to time and at all times freely have and fully enjoy his or their Judgments or Consciencyes in matters of Religion throughout all the province, they behaving themselves peaceably and quietly and not useing this Liberty to Lycentiousnesse nor to the civil Injury or outward disturbance of others...

*Laws of the Colony of New York* (Albany, 1894), I, 115

# The Glorious Revolution of 1688

The Glorious Revolution of 1688 in England put an end to this brief period of religious toleration in New York. When news of the revolution reached the colony, it led to a populist rebellion by the fiercely anti-Catholic Jacob Leisler.

Order was restored, but the new royal governor, the Earl of Bellomont, was as anti-Catholic as Leisler. In 1696 he reported happily that only nine Catholics were known to exist in New York. In 1700 the colonial assembly passed "An Act against Jesuits and Popish Priests," which described Catholic priests as enemies "to the true Christian religion." Any Catholic priest entering the colony was subject to arrest and life imprisonment. Any priest who escaped and was recaptured was liable to the death penalty. Anyone giving shelter to a Popish priest was liable to a fine of 200 pounds. As in contemporary England and Ireland, Catholics were forbidden to vote, hold public office or serve on juries. Eighteenth-century New York was a wasteland for Catholics. An incident in 1741 illustrated how easy it was to arouse the latent anti-Catholicism of the populace. In that year there was an abortive rebellion of black slaves in New York City. Rumors circulated that the rebellion was part of a Spanish Catholic plot. John Ury, a non-juring Anglican clergyman, was accused of complicity in the alleged conspiracy and executed as a Popish priest. By the 1770's or the 1780's, however, there must have been at least a few Catholics in New York City, because we know that they were visited occasionally by a German-born Jesuit from Pennsylvania, Father Ferdinand Steinmeyer (a.k.a. "Father Farmer"), who celebrated Mass for them in secret. Organized Catholic life, however, would have to wait until the dawn of a better day.

## AN ACT AGAINST JESUITS & POPISH PREISTS
## AUGUST 9, 1700

And be it further Enacted by the authority aforesaid, that all and every Jesuit Seminary Preist Missionary or other Spirituall or Ecclesiasticall person made or Ordained by any Authority power or Jurisdiction derived Challenged or p'tended from the pope or See of Rome or that shall profess himself or otherwise appear to be Such by preaching & teaching of others to Say any popish prayers by Celebrating masses granting of absolutions or using any other of the Romish Ceremonies & Rites of worship by what name title or degree so ever such person shall be called or known who shall Continue abide remaine or come into this province or any part thereof after the first day of November aforesaid shall be deemed and Accounted an incendiary and disturber of the public peace and Safety and an Enemy to the true Christian Religion and shall be adjudged to Suffer perpetual Imprisonm't and if any person being So Sentenced and actually Imprisoned shall break prison and make his Escape and be afterwards retaken he shall Suffer such paines of Death penalties and forfeitures as in Cases of felony.

*Laws of the Colony of New York* (Albany, 1894), I, 428-429

Plan of New Amsterdam, 1660

# Catholics
## AND THE AMERICAN REVOLUTION

During the Revolutionary War anti-Catholic bigotry, which had been pervasive throughout the colonial period, virtually disapeared. One reason for this happy development was the fact that Catholic France and Spain were the colonists' principal allies. Another reason was the fact that most American Catholics seem to have supported the Patriot cause. To be sure, the American Catholic role in the Revolution was minimal, for they numbered no more than one percent of the entire population.

Nonetheless, in Maryland, Charles Carroll of Carrolltown, reputedly the richest man in the colonies, risked both his wealth and his life to sign the Declaration of Independence. In Philadelphia, the first urban Catholic center in the Thirteen Colonies, merchants Stephen Moylan and George Meade provided material assistance to the war effort while sea captain John Barry saw action in several naval engagements against the British, thus establishing a claim to be called the Father of the U.S. Navy.

Perhaps the best known example of Catholic support for the Revolution occurred in 1776 when Charles Carroll and his cousin Father John Carroll accompanied Benjamin Franklin and Samuel Chase on their trip to Canada in an unsuccessful effort to persuade the French Canadians to join the American revolt against Great Britain. John Carroll later had misgivings about the role that he played on that occasion, not that he regretted his support of the Patriot cause, but he wondered about the wisdom of a cleric involving himself directly in political affairs. "When the ministers of religion leave the duties of their profession to take a busy part in political matters," he observed, "they generally fall into contempt and sometimes even bring discredit to the cause in whose service they are engaged."

Archbishop John Carroll, 1735-1815

In the spring of 1776, on his way north to Canada, John Carroll stopped briefly in New York City and described the feverish preparations then under way to fortify the city against an imminent British attack. "When we came to New York," he told his mother, "it was no more the gay, polite place it used to be esteemed, but was become almost a desert, except for the troops. The people were expecting a bombardment, and had therefore removed themselves and their effects out of town..." American efforts to defend New York proved fruitless, however, and George Washington retreated south with the Continental Army. The British captured the city in November 1776 and occupied it for the rest of the war.

The *Royal Gazette,* a Tory newspaper published in occupied New York, made a crude appeal to anti-Catholic prejudice with a report in January 1780 that Spanish ships were on their way to America with a cargo that included "50 tons of holy water... 400 casks of consecrated oil for extreme unction; 10,000 cuts of various saints with brief accounts of the miracles worked by their reliques and at their shrines; 20,000 hair shirts, cowls and scourges... 3,000 wheels, hooks, pincers, knives, shackles and fire brands for the use of the Inquisition; 10,000 copies of a treatise entitled *Wholesome Reveries, or the Necessity of Extirpating Heretics.*" If the Tories tried to inflame anti-Catholic feeling, the Patriots did their best to discourage it. On four separate occasions Congress attended services at St. Mary's Church in Philadelphia, and George Washington issued an order to his soldiers, forbidding them from celebrating Guy Fawkes Day by hanging effigies of the pope.

## Catholics in the New Republic

Sanctuary of St. Peter's Church, New York's first Catholic Parish, founded 1785

In 1783, when Great Britain admitted defeat and formally recognized the independence of the United States, American Catholics could hardly believe their good fortune. Writing to Rome that year, a group of American priests said: "Our religious system has undergone a revolution, if possible, more extraordinary than our political one."

In all thirteen states Catholics now enjoyed full religious freedom although only five states gave them full civil rights. In New York, for example, the state constitution of 1777 contained a provision that required office holders to repudiate all foreign allegiances, "ecclesiastical as well as civil." The stipulation had deliberately been inserted in the state constitution to bar Catholics from holding public office. It was the work of John Jay, the bitterly anti-Catholic descendant of Huguenot refugees who had originally been welcomed to New York by the enlightened Catholic colonial governor Thomas Dongan. The offensive legislation was not removed until 1806 when it was challenged by the first Catholic elected to the state legislature, Francis Cooper.

Independence created challenges as well as opportunities for American Catholics. One immediate problem was the question of ecclesiastical jurisdiction. For many years the vicar apostolic of the London District had exercised a shadowy authority over the Church in the Thirteen Colonies. After 1783 such subordination to an English bishop was neither practical nor desirable. Instead the American priests, who numbered no more than two dozen, petitioned the Holy See to appoint one of them as the superior of the Catholic Church in the new Republic. The priests emphasized that they wanted only a priest as their superior, not a bishop, for fear that the appointment of a bishop would provoke a resurgence of anti-Catholic bigotry.

In reponse the Roman authorities obliged the American clergy by appointing one of them as Superior of the Mission, the canonical equivalent of a prefect apostolic. However, they did not select for the post the candidate of the American priests, John Lewis. At age sixty-three, Lewis was declared too old and in need of "repose rather than arduous labor." Instead, at the suggestion of Benjamin Franklin, minister at the French court, the appointment went to John Carroll, who had been Franklin's companion on the ill-fated diplomatic mission to Canada in 1776. From the Roman point of view, the most surprising development was the attitude of the American government when it was consulted by the Holy See about the appointment of Carroll. The American officials politely replied that it was a purely religious matter, and that the Holy See was therefore free to do whatever it pleased. As the Roman authorities were well aware, there was no Catholic country in the world that would have given the Church such freedom of action.

When the British finally evacuated New York on November 25, 1783, they left behind a demoralized population whose numbers had shrunk to 10,000. The population more than doubled over the next few years, however, due mainly to an influx of newcomers from rural New England and Ireland.

In 1784 the Anti-Priest Law of 1700 was repealed, giving the local Catholic community the opportunity to organize the first Catholic parish in New York. Catholic New York consisted of 200 or 300 people, most of them poor, many of them "grumblers" (according to the first pastor), but several of them men of considerable wealth.

Among the latter were Dominic Lynch and his business partner Thomas Stoughton, both merchants and importers; Andrew Morris, a wealthy chandler; William Mooney, an upholsterer who would later become the first Grand Sachem of the Tammany Society; and Hector St. John de Crèvecœur, the French consul. The lay leaders incorporated "The Roman Catholic Church in the City of New York" on June 10, 1785, and four months later they purchased from Trinity Episcopal Church property at the corner of Church and Barclay Streets. There, on October 5, 1785, they laid the cornerstone for New York's first Catholic church, St. Peter's. The unfinished little frame building was dedicated on November 4, 1786.

Unfortunately, it proved to be easier to build a church than to find a satisfactory pastor for the congregation. St. Peter's first shepherd was Father Charles Whelan, an Irish Capuchin who arrived by chance in New York in October 1784. A year later another wandering Irish Capuchin appeared on the scene, Father Andrew Nugent. The two friars quarreled with one another and divided the congregation. Whelan resigned in disgust in February 1786, whereupon Nugent became embroiled in a bitter dispute with the lay trustees over money.

Such conflicts between priests and lay trustees were a common feature of American Catholicism in that era and were aggravated by the lack a bishop with authority to settle such disputes. As the Superior of the Mission, it fell to Carroll to try to settle the conflict in New York. Twice he was barred from celebrating Mass in St. Peter's Church by partisans of Nugent. Finally, with the help of the civil authorities, he wrested control of St. Peter's from Nugent and in October 1787 installed as pastor an Irish Dominican, William V. O'Brien.

Exterior of St. Peter's Church, Barclay Street

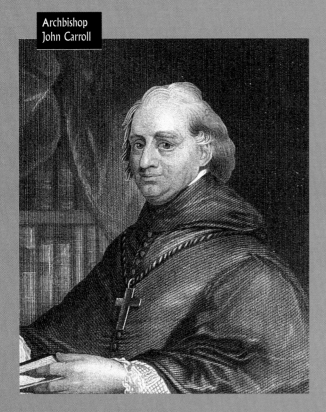

Archbishop John Carroll

Carroll's unhappy experiences in New York convinced him that the time had come for the appointment of an American Catholic bishop. The American priests, who in 1784 had resisted such a step from fear of an anti-Catholic backlash, had also come to the same conclusion. In March 1788 they told Pope Pius VI: "We find more and more under the very liberal constitution of the Republic, that if among the clergy there are some men of intractable character, who are restive under ecclesiastical discipline, they offer as the reason for their unruliness and disobedience that they are bound to obey a bishop who wields personal authority, but not a simple priest who has only delegated authority... This was recently done in New York by those who wished to throw off the yoke of authority."

The Holy Father agreed about the need for an American bishop and allowed the American clergy to choose one of their own for the post. The priests voted for Carroll by a margin of twenty-four to two; Rome approved the nomination, and John Carroll was

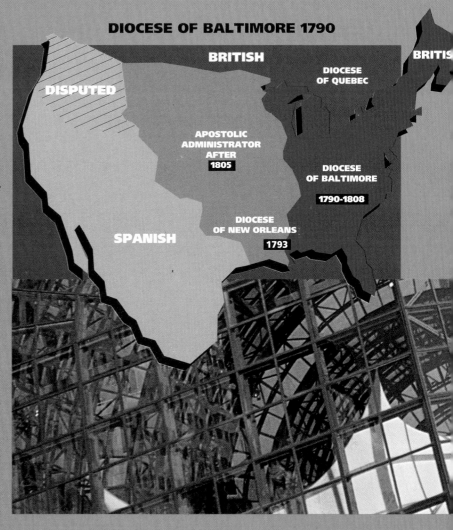

### DIOCESE OF BALTIMORE 1790

BRITISH

BRITIS

DISPUTED

DIOCESE OF QUEBEC

APOSTOLIC ADMINISTRATOR AFTER 1805

DIOCESE OF BALTIMORE

1790-1808

SPANISH

DIOCESE OF NEW ORLEANS

1793

appointed Bishop of Baltimore on November 6, 1789. For his consecration he travelled to England, and, on August 15, 1790, he received episcopal orders from Bishop James Walmesley at Lulworth Castle in Dorsetshire, the country estate of Thomas Weld, England's largest Catholic landowner.

Carroll returned to the United States to assume control of a diocese that was coterminous with the country, which meant that in effect John Carroll of Baltimore was really New York's first bishop. During the nineteen years that Carroll was the country's sole ordinary (1789-1808), the whole state of New York could boast of only two parishes, St. Peter's Church in New York City, and St. Mary's Church in Albany. The latter church was opened in 1798, one year after Albany replaced New York City as the state capital and, more significantly, one year after New York City replaced Philadelphia as the country's busiest port.

# Diocese

## OF NEW YORK

On April 8, 1808, John Carroll was made the Archbishop of Baltimore, and his original diocese was divided into four suffragan sees, one of which was the Diocese of New York. Pope Pius VII accepted Carroll's nominees for Boston, Philadelphia and Bardstown.

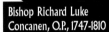

Bishop Richard Luke Concanen, O.P., 1747-1810

In the case of New York, however, Carroll had no one to recommend. "Amongst the clergy of that state, " he said, "there was none whom my judgment approved as fit for it." Therefore, he asked the Holy Father to leave New York vacant and to place it temporarily under the jurisdiction of the Bishop of Boston. The Pope, however, decided otherwise. He appointed as the first Bishop of New York Richard Luke Concanen, a sixty-one year old Irish Dominican who had lived in Rome since 1765.

It was not an especially happy choice, and Archbishop Carroll spent the next two years waiting for Bishop Concanen to cross the Atlantic and visit his diocese. The new bishop made several unsuccessful attempts to sail directly from Italy to America, but it was exceptionally dangerous and difficult for a British subject like Concanen to hazard such a voyage during the naval war between France and England.

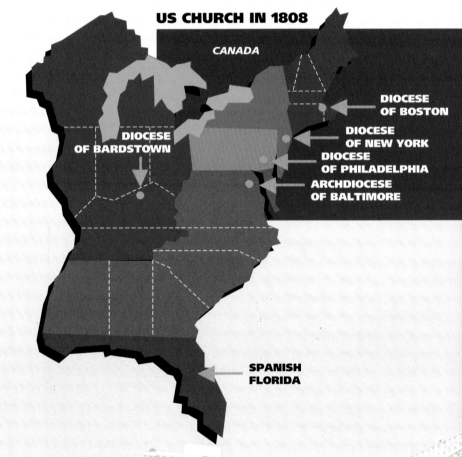

US CHURCH IN 1808

CANADA

DIOCESE
OF BOSTON

DIOCESE
OF NEW YORK

DIOCESE
OF PHILADELPHIA

ARCHDIOCESE
OF BALTIMORE

DIOCESE
OF BARDSTOWN

SPANISH
FLORIDA

However, Concanen's own Dominican confreres in Rome seemed to think that he could have made a more determined effort than he did to reach his diocese. Without a doubt, so did M. Jacques Bénigne Emery, the rector of the Seminary of St. Sulpice in Paris and the legendary leader of the French clergy during the worst years of the Revolution. "He adds affliction to the afflicted," said Concanen, when informed of Emery's criticism.

Eventually Archbishop Carroll tried to interest Concanen in taking an alternative route to America. Through the intervention of Emery and Cardinal Joseph Fesch (Napoleon's uncle),

Carroll obtained a safe conduct pass for Concanen to travel through France and embark on any American "public dispatch vessel" sailing from French ports. Nevertheless, Bishop Concanen still tarried in Rome, complaining of poor health (he may have been suffering from cancer) and lack of money and wondering where to purchase the "dozen pair of purple silk stockings" requested by Carroll.

Meanwhile, Carroll at least prevailed upon Concanen to send him copies

Carroll had still another motive for wanting to see the Bishop of New York. "How earnestly do I now wish for Bishop Concanen's arrival," he said in the spring of that year. "He will probably bring some instructions... as to the conduct to be pursued by the first pastors (i.e., the bishops) of the Church." On June 19, 1810, however, Bishop Concanen died suddenly in Naples after making one last

Dominican Church in Naples, burial site of Bishop Concanen

of the papal bulls establishing the Archdiocese of Baltimore and the four new suffragan sees. The documents arrived safely in America, thanks to another newly-appointed bishop, Benedict Flaget of Bardstown, who crossed the Atlantic twice while Concanen was considering his travel options.

After Napoleon's abduction and imprisonment of the Pope in 1810,

futile attempt to book passage to America. Thus New York never saw its first bishop, and John Carroll never got his dozen pair of purple silk stockings.

For the next four years Pope Pius VII remained a prisoner of Napoleon. The pontiff retaliated with the only weapon available to him. He went on strike and refused to appoint any new bishops until

he was released from captivity. From 1810 to 1815, therefore, the Diocese of New York was deliberately left vacant. Fortunately, in July 1808, Concanen had authorized Carroll to appoint a vicar general in New York. Carroll picked for the post Anthony Kohlmann, an Alsatian-born Jesuit, whom he had already decided to send there.

# Anthony Kohlmann, S. J.

In February 1807, Carroll had asked the Jesuits for Kohlmann's services in New York "to prevent the explosion of dreadful scandals there." Kohlmann arrived in the city in the fall of 1808 and confirmed Carroll's gloomy assessment of the situation. "The scandals given in this congregation," he said, "have brought it very near its ruin." It is not clear what was the exact nature of these scandals, but Kohlmann's first responsibility was to reestablish stability at St. Peter's Church where both the pastor (the Dominican William O'Brien) and the curate (Matthew O'Brien) had departed during the previous year.

New York Literary Institute, 1808-1813

St. Patrick's Old Cathedral, dedicated in 1815

Kohlmann also intended to establish a Jesuit school in New York. He had brought with him for this purpose Father Benedict Fenwick (a Maryland-born Jesuit and future Bishop of Boston) and four Jesuit scholastics. With their help by Christmas of 1808 he had founded the New York Literary Institute. Located first on Mulberry Street and then on the site of the present cathedral, it was New York's first Catholic "college." After a promising beginning, which saw the school grow to some forty boarders and even enroll the son of the governor of New York, the institution was closed in 1813 by the Jesuits who wished to concentrate their limited resources in Georgetown College.

Kohlmann was also responsible for the erection of New York's City second Catholic church, St. Patrick's Old Cathedral, at Prince and Mott Streets, which was begun on June 8, 1809, and was dedicated by Bishop John Cheverus of Boston on May 4, 1815. Kohlmann also achieved fame because of his connection with a lawsuit involving the seal of confession. A penitent had used Kohlmann as an intermediary to make restitution, and Kohlmann refused to reveal the man's identity. The district attorney wished to drop the case, but the Catholics of the city insisted that it should go to trial in order to obtain a clear-cut decision. Their tactics paid off handsomely, for the court declared: "If

The college is in the center not of Long Island but of the Island of New York, the most delightful and healthy spot of the whole island, at a distance of four small miles from the city, and of half a mile from the East and North rivers, both of which are seen from the house; situated between two roads which are very much frequented... Every one thinks that, if the reputation of the house is kept up, it will in a short time rivalize any college in this country. I expect we shall have thirty boarders for the beginning of next month.

This city will always be the first city in America on account of its advantageous situation for commerce. From the West Indies parents will send their children to this port in preference to any other. The professors of the State's or Columbia College have sent us these two years past a kind invitation to accompany, at what they call the annual commencement, the procession of the students from the college to some or other church, where speeches are delivered and degrees conferred; they had never paid that attention to the Catholic clergy before.

Anthony Kohlmann, S.J., to the Reverend Mr. Strickland, S.J., September 14, 1810. *Historical Records and Studies* I, Part 1 (January 1899), 73.

Bishop John Connolly, O.P., 1747-1825

(Kohlmann) tells the truth, he violates his judicial oath... The only course is for the court to declare that he shall not testify or act at all."

Between 1808 and 1815, the first seven years of the Diocese of New York, all four of the priests engaged in parochial ministry were Jesuits. Unfortunately, the other two were not of the same caliber as Kohlmann and Fenwick. Peter Anthony Malou was a former Belgian general whose cantankerous personality eventually led to his expulsion from the Society and his suspension from the diocese. Father Maximilan Rantzau, who replaced Kohlmann in 1815, was a sickly individual with a limited command of English.

Two others religious orders made brief appearances in the diocese. In the spring of 1812 three Irish Ursulines arrived in New York and inaugurated a girl's academy which lasted until 1815. In 1814 five Trappists, refugees from the French Revolution, came to New York hoping to establish a monastery in the former New York Literary Institute.

Their plans foundered for financial reasons, and in the spring of 1815, the last French Trappists sailed out of New York harbor in the same ship as the Irish Ursulines.

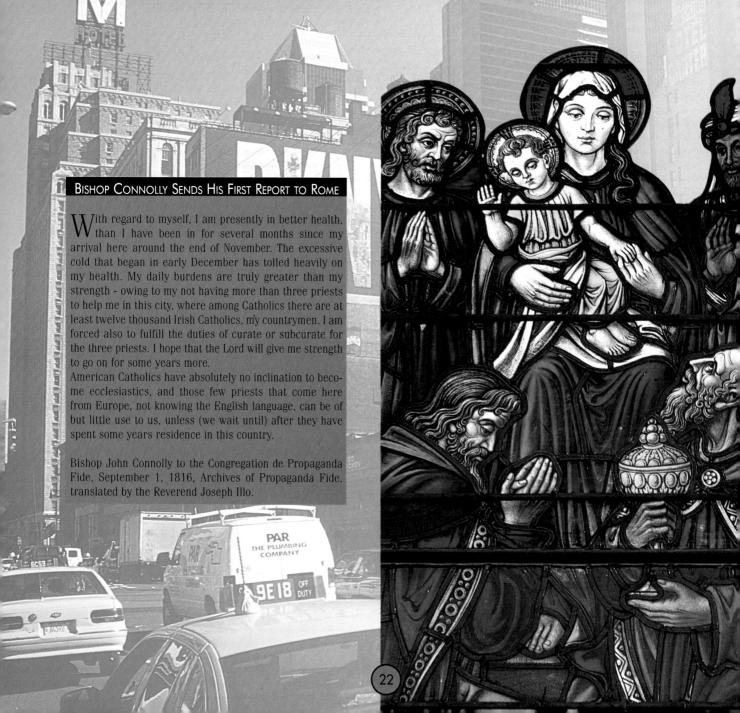

That summer Carroll heard rumors that a new Bishop of New York had been appointed and consecrated in Rome, another elderly Irish Dominican without any pastoral experience, John Connolly. In the course of the summer of 1815, rumor became fact, but Bishop Connolly still failed to make an appearance in New York, and Archbishop Carroll grew increasingly apprehensive. He complained to the Roman authorities about the delay and told them that Bishop Connolly's arrival was "eagerly awaited by me and by his flock."

Carroll was also annoyed about the manner of Connolly's appointment. For the second time in seven years Rome had appointed a bishop in New York without consulting him or anyone else in the United States. "I wish this may not become a very dangerous precedent," he said, "fruitful of mischief by drawing censure upon our religion and false opinion of the servility of our principles."

Archbishop Carroll was now in his eightieth year. His health began to fail that summer as he anxiously awaited the news of Connolly's

arrival in New York so that he could relinquish at least that part of his responsibilities. By mid-October Bishop Connolly had still not come, although Carroll heard reports that he had reached Liège. A few weeks later Carroll became seriously ill, and it was obvious that he was not likely to recover. Still there was no word from Bishop Connolly. On November 23, 1815, Carroll received the last rites. The next day Connolly landed in New York. Ten days later John Carroll of Baltimore was dead.

## BISHOP CONNOLLY SENDS HIS FIRST REPORT TO ROME

With regard to myself, I am presently in better health, than I have been in for several months since my arrival here around the end of November. The excessive cold that began in early December has tolled heavily on my health. My daily burdens are truly greater than my strength - owing to my not having more than three priests to help me in this city, where among Catholics there are at least twelve thousand Irish Catholics, my countrymen. I am forced also to fulfill the duties of curate or subcurate for the three priests. I hope that the Lord will give me strength to go on for some years more.

American Catholics have absolutely no inclination to become ecclesiastics, and those few priests that come here from Europe, not knowing the English language, can be of but little use to us, unless (we wait until) after they have spent some years residence in this country.

Bishop John Connolly to the Congregation de Propaganda Fide, September 1, 1816, Archives of Propaganda Fide, translated by the Reverend Joseph Illo.

# Bishop John Connolly, O.P.

It has been said of Bishop Connolly (by historian Peter Guilday) that "it may well be doubted if, in the history of the Catholic Church in the United States, any other bishop began his episcopal life under such disheartening conditions." At the age of sixty-eight, he found himself unexpectedly shipped across the Atlantic to take charge of a chaotic missionary diocese of 55,000 square miles.

He had at his disposal three churches (two in New York City and one in Albany) and six priests. Of the six priests, two were Jesuits (Fenwick and Rantzau) who were soon assigned elsewhere; the third was the impossible Malou whom he suspended; the fourth was an ambitious Irish Dominican (Thomas Carbry) who was angling for a mitre; the fifth was the pastor in Albany, a clerical *oiseau de passage* who soon flew home to Canada.

The sixth priest was Michael O'Gorman, a graduate of St. Kieran's College, Kilkenny, whom Connolly had ordained in Ireland at the age of twenty-three and had brought with him to America as New York's first diocesan priest. O'Gorman's brief career is indicative of the burdens of the New York clergy of that era. Connolly immediately sent O'Gorman to the new cathedral that Kohlmann had built. In 1817 Connolly made O'Gorman pastor of St. Mary's Church in Albany from where he traveled regularly along the route of the Erie Canal as far west as Utica and Auburn, ministering to the needs of the canal workers and their families. He was the first priest ever to celebrate Mass in Auburn, using the

Letter of Bishop Connolly to Archbishop Carroll, New York, February 13, 1817, mentioning that the trustees have not paid his salary for three months

local court house for the occasion. In 1819 Connolly recalled O'Gorman to help him in the cathedral.

Five years later, the aging bishop asked Rome to appoint O'Gorman as his coadjutor and successor. The Roman authorities wrote back to remind Connolly that he was supposed to submit three names, not one, for the post of coadjutor. At that point, however, the niceties of canon law did not make much difference to poor Father O'Gorman, for he died on November 18, 1824, at the age of thirty-two, after nine years of service as New York's first diocesan priest. Eight days later Connolly lost another young priest, Richard Bulger, like O'Gorman a native of Kilkenny and the first priest actually ordained in New York. He had been a priest for only four years.

# The Rise of the Port of New York

Connolly's ten years as bishop coincided with the construction of the Erie Canal, which was begun in 1817 and completed in 1825. The 363-mile, 83-lock canal connected the Great Lakes with the Atlantic and confirmed New York City's reputation as the premier East Coast port. By 1825 the Port of New York was already handling almost half of the country's imports and a third of its exports. With the completion of the Erie Canal, the growth of New York broke all previous records. By 1830 the population of the city was 200,000. During the next thirty years it quadrupled, and by 1860 New York City contained more people than Baltimore, Philadelphia and Boston combined.

## THE DIOCESE OF NEW YORK IN 1822

### BISHOPRIC OF NEW-YORK.

Rt. Rev'd. Dr. John Connolly, Bishop.

THE bishopric of New-York, comprehends the whole state of New-York, together with the northern parts of Jersey. The residence of the Bishop is in New-York. This city contains two Catholic Churches, viz: the Cathedral (St. Patrick's) and St. Peters.

The Cathedral is a superb edifice, 120 feet long by 80 feet wide, finished in a superior manner in the inside, and is capable of holding 6000 people. The exterior, as to the ornamental part, is yet unfinished. The style of the building is Gothic; and from its great extent and solidity, must have cost upwards of 90,000 dollars. No church in the United States, (the Cathedral in Baltimore excepted) can compare with it.

St. Peter's, which is the first Catholic Church erected in New-York, is a neat, convenient, and handsome building. It was erected about 20 years ago, at which time the number of Catholics did not exceed three hundred. At present they number upwards of twenty thousand. They are mostly natives of Ireland and France.

There are in this city two extensive Catholic charity schools, conducted upon a judicious plan, and supported partly by the funds of the state, and partly by moneys raised twice a year by the two congregations. Independently of these two establishments, the Emittsburg sisters of charity have a branch here of their pious institution, exclusively for the benefit of female orphan children, whom they board, clothe and educate. Their house fronts the side of the Cathedral, and is in one of the most healthy situations in New-York.

In Albany there is likewise a Catholic church—a neat and compact building. It was erected about 14 years ago, and is attended by a growing congregation. The clergyman officiating in this church, visits occasionally Troy, Lansingbugh, Johnstown and Schenectady.

In Utica, a large and beautiful church has lately been erected and consecrated, which reflects great honour on the Catholics residing there. Their number is not great; neither are they generally wealthy—their zeal however *for the house of God, and the place where his glory dwelleth*, has enabled them to surmount every obstacle to the exercise of their piety. From the multitude flocking annually to this flourishing village, no doubt can be entertained but this will shortly become one of the most numerous, and respectable congregations in the diocess.

In Rome, (15 miles distant from Utica,) there is as yet no Catholic church, but a beautiful lot is reserved, by the liberality of Dominick Lynch, Esq. on which one will be erected, as soon as the number of Catholics settling there will render its erection necessary. The situation of this little town is healthy and beautiful.

In Auburn, an agreeable little town, still farther distant in the state, there is likewise a Catholic church, recently erected.

In New-Jersey, in the town of Patterson, there is also one, which is regularly attended by a clergyman.

In Carthage, near the Black River, a small and neat church has been lately erected.

### THE FOLLOWING ARE THE CATHOLIC CLERGYMEN OFFICIATING IN THIS DIOCESS.

#### NEW-YORK.

Rt. Rev'd. Dr. John Connolly, } St. Patrick's Cathe-
Rev. Michael O'Gorman, } dral.
Rev'd. Charles French, } St. Peter's.
Rev'd. John Power, }
Rev'd. Mr. Bulger, Patterson.
Rev'd. Michael Carroll, Albany and vicinity.
Rev'd. John Farnan, Utica and vicinity.
Rev'd. Patrick Kelly, Auburn, Rochester, and other districts in the Western parts of this state.
Rev'd. Philip Larissy attends regularly at Staten-Island, and different other congregations along the Hudson River.

The Laity's Directory to the Church Service for the Year of Our Lord, M, DCCC, XXII (New York, 1822), pp. 104-106

As Robert Albion pointed out fifty years ago in his classic study of the port of New York, the prosperity of the city was not due solely to the Erie Canal. An equally important factor was the fact that ambitious New York businessmen had succeeded in monopolizing most of the cotton trade between the southern states and Europe. "By creating a three-cornered trade in the cotton triangle," Albion said, "New York dragged the commerce between the Southern ports and Europe out of its normal course some two hundred miles to collect heavy toll upon it."

Added to this was the fact that New York businessmen also developed a lucrative coastal trade. Also beginning in the 1820's, New York was the first American city to offer regularly scheduled packet service to England. As a result, said Albion,

"this meant that, except for the immediate spheres of influence of Boston, Philadelphia and Baltimore, most of the country had become New York's hinterland at least two decades before the Civil War." New York became so important economically that for years the import duties collected at the New York Custom House practically financed the federal government. In 1828, for example, the import duties collected there "were enough to finance the whole running expenses of the national government, except the interest on the debt."

Not only did New York outstrip all of its maritime rivals in the years before the Civil War, but it also became the largest manufactuing center in the United States. In the opinion of Sean Wilentz, "by the 1840's (it) was probably the fastest-growing large industrial area in the world." Between 1800 and 1850

the rate of growth was 750%, higher than that of Liverpool or Manchester or - in Wilentz's words, "higher than that of all the jerry-built catastrophes of Dickensian lore." In the 1820's the newcomers who were flooding into the city came mainly from rural New England or upstate New York, supplemented by a substantial number of Protestant immigrants from the British Isles. In 1825 New York was still an overwhelmingly Protestant city with three Catholic churches and 99 Protestant churches. In the 1830's, however, a major change took place in the pattern of European immigration to New York. In that decade, for the first time, the city began to see the arrival of large numbers of Irish Catholics and Germans (many of whom were also Catholic).

# The Immigrant
## CHURCH

Many of the Irish immigrants who arrived before 1830 were "two-boaters," that is, they travelled first from Ireland to Canada (often in the timber ships that left Ireland every spring), then took a second ship from Canada to the United States. Such was the itinerary of the parents of James Cardinal Gibbons and many other Irish immigrants of the early nineteenth century. Boston first became a magnet for Irish immigrants because of its proximity to Canada.

Others traveled farther south to New York, drawn by the prospect of work on the Erie Canal, which was dug by hand, largely by Irish immigrant laborers, who were paid approximately fifty cents a day. By 1825 it is estimated that there were about 50,000 Irish living along the route of the canal, not only laborers, but also quarrymen, saltmakers, farmers, and a nascent middle class of contractors and sub-contractors, who created a string of Catholic communities from Albany to Buffalo. Bishop Connolly tried to provide for their spiritual needs by sending them young priests like Father O'Gorman and Father Bulger to establish parishes in Utica, Syracuse, Auburn, Rochester, Carthage and other upstate communities. Unfortunately, the demand for priests far outstripped Connolly's ability to supply them.

Many of the Irish immigrants remained where they landed, in New York City. In 1820 they already numbered about 20,000; by 1845, on the eve of the Great Famine in Ireland, there were approximately 70,000 Irish in New York City. Most were unskilled or semi-skilled workers who found employment as day laborers, stage-coach drivers, construction workers or longshoremen. They frequently lived in appalling poverty in the slums of the 4th, 5th, and 6th wards of lower Manhattan where rickety tenements without adequate light or sanitation stood next to slaughter houses, stables and breweries. Crime and alcoholism were rampant. In the 6th ward it was said that there was one grog shop for every six inhabitants. Unlike later generations of Irish Catholic immigrants, those who came to the United States before the Great Famine of the 1840's were not notably consistent churchgoers. Probably no more than 40 % to 60 % of them attended Sunday Mass on a regular basis. Later in the century, Monsignor Richard Burstell, a prominent New York City pastor, commented:"Half of our Irish population here is Catholic merely because Catholicity was the religion of the land of their birth."

The Irish who did come to their parish church on Sunday were likely to attend one of several Low Masses that was said inaudibly in Latin and took no more than a half-hour to complete. It should be remembered that they came from a country where the Catholic Church was just emerging from the catacombs after centuries of persecution and where it was not even legal until 1822 to ring the Angelus bell. It is small wonder then that Irish-American understanding of liturgy was (in the words of Walter Elliott) "catacombical." One of the most noticeable features of Catholic devotional life was the prominence given to frequent reception of the sacrament of penance."More than anything else," said Jay Dolan, the historian of antebellum New York Catholicism,"this emphasis on confession stands out as a dominant feature of religious life among the Catholics, especially the Irish."

Although historians may wonder about the Mass attendance of the pre-famine Irish immigrants, there can be no doubt about their generosity to the Church. It has been said that "the building of the Roman Catholic Church was the greatest collective achievement of the Irish in the United States." The Irish possessed advantages that many of the other Catholic immigrants lacked, such as familiarity with the English language and with the principle of voluntary financial support of the Church. They were also accustomed to anti-Catholic prejudice and to using political power to combat such prejudice. For all these reasons, said Lawrence McCaffrey, "the Irish were the only Catholic group that could have led an American Catholic Church with a diverse European immigrant constituency into an accommodation with the dominant, Anglo-American Protestant culture."

N. Y. Weekly Register.

SATURDAY, NOVEMBER 16, 1833.

IRISH SERVANTS IN NEW-YORK.

Our attention has, for some time past, been directed to the many privations and obstructions in their religious duties, experienced by this very useful portion of our civic population. There is, with few exceptions, no class in the community, which contributes more largely to domestic comfort. From their acknowledged habits of industry, cleanliness, sobriety, and honesty, the Irish servants are rapidly rising in the estimation of the discerning portion of our fellow-citizens. Now and then, indeed, we meet a stray article, fraught with ill-natured reflections, thrown out in the columns of some fanatical journal, hostile to the character of our country : but as experience has taught the American public, that all such insinuations are ever found to be the overflowings of ignorance or prejudice, they are, at this enlightened period, regarded as altogether innocuous. Those stupid railers ought, for their own sakes, at least, learn better manners : for were it not owing to the continued immigration of Irish servants, there's not "a mother's soul of them," that should not become " cook, slut and butler" to himself :—servants could not, in fact, be procured on any terms.

But while, in spite of some local prejudice and much religious bigotry, the utility, not to say, the indispensableness, of Irish servants is now generally conceded; we should be the more anxious, that all the privileges to which they are entitled, by the equitable laws of our Republic, should be inviolably preserved. I is well known, that almost all the Irish servants are Catholics. They come hither under the fullest conviction, that it is a land o liberty ; in which every one can worship God according as conscience dictates :—a land in which toleration, in its utmost extent, is paramount. What then must be the disappointment of these simple-hearted creatures, when they find, that so far from being in a land of freedom in religious concerns, they are not unfrequently required to have a creed, always conformable to that of the pious family in which they happen to live! In a country containing so many and so multiform shades of belief, this chameleon-like mode of saying their *Pater* and *Aves* must be rather inconvenient.

New York Weekly Register and Catholic Diary, November 16, 1833, describes the difficulties of Irish Catholic servants in New York

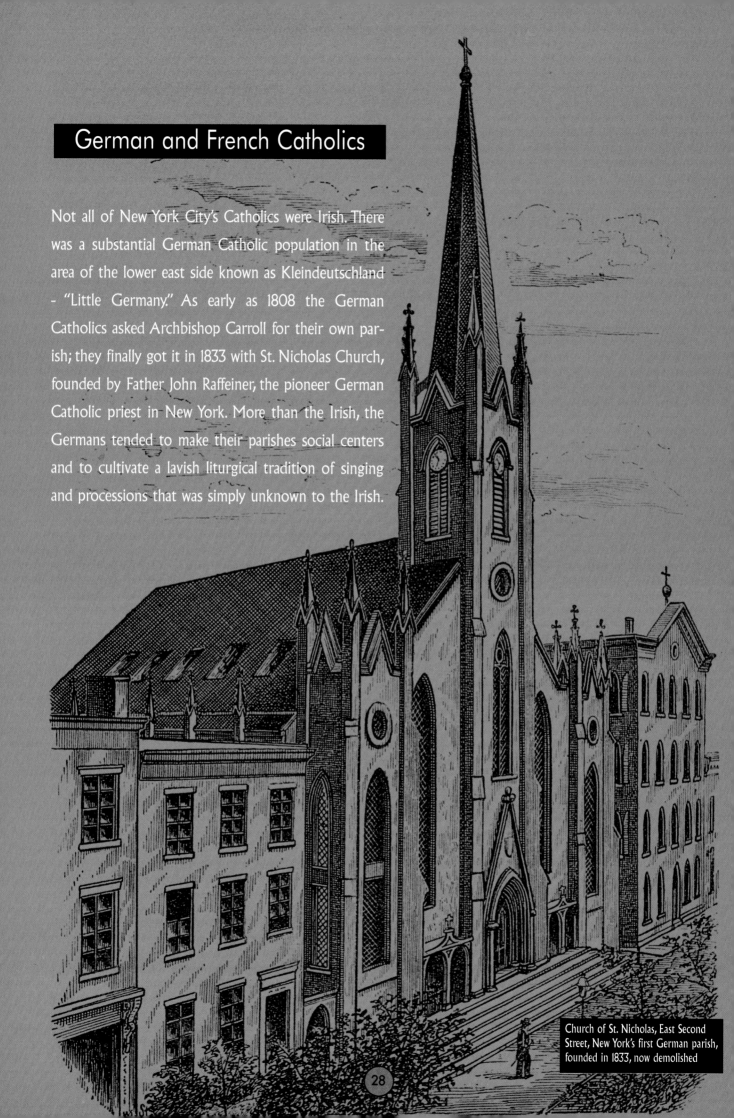

# German and French Catholics

Not all of New York City's Catholics were Irish. There was a substantial German Catholic population in the area of the lower east side known as Kleindeutschland - "Little Germany." As early as 1808 the German Catholics asked Archbishop Carroll for their own parish; they finally got it in 1833 with St. Nicholas Church, founded by Father John Raffeiner, the pioneer German Catholic priest in New York. More than the Irish, the Germans tended to make their parishes social centers and to cultivate a lavish liturgical tradition of singing and processions that was simply unknown to the Irish.

Church of St. Nicholas, East Second Street, New York's first German parish, founded in 1833, now demolished

They also tended to be clannish, desiring their own parochial schools, hospitals, orphanages, Catholic newspaper and even separate German Catholic cemeteries. Another characteristic of New York's German parishes was the number that were administered by religious orders, most notably the Redemptorists, who in 1844 founded Most Holy Redeemer Church on East 3rd Street. In 1851 they replaced the original wooden structure with a massive rococo church which could accommodate 3,500 worshippers.

In 1847 the Redemptorists opened another German parish, St. Alphonsus on Thompson Street. When the Irish Catholics in the area began to frequent St. Alphonsus, they were provided with a Sunday Mass of their own in the basement of the Church. However, the enterprising pastor soon discovered that the Irish were more generous contributors to the collection than the Germans. He thereupon switched the "English" Mass to the upper church, much to the indignation of the German parishioners, who said: "We will not go downstairs and have the Irish over our heads."

For a brief period in the 1790's and early 1800's New York's City was also host to 3,000 to 4,000 French-speaking immigrants, refugees from the Revolution in France and in Saint Domingue (Haiti). Most of them departed after the downfall of Napoleon, but a few lingered on to form the nucleus of a French Catholic community that was sufficiently numerous in 1841 to establish their own parish of St. Vincent de Paul. The most famous member of this French-speaking community was not a Frenchman at all, but a black slave from Saint Domingue, Pierre Toussaint, who came to New York in 1787, was emancipated in 1807 and became a prosperous hairdresser. A property-owner and pew holder in St. Peter's Church, Toussaint was well known for his generosity to the poor, especially the children in the Catholic orphan asylum.

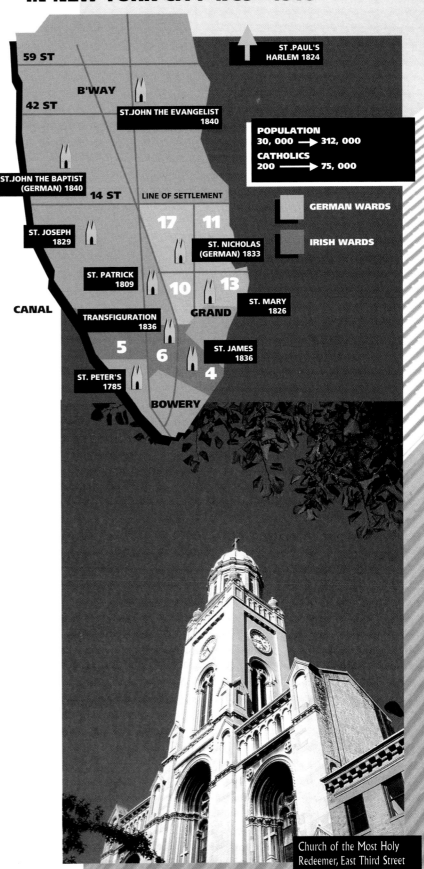

## CATHOLIC CHURCHES IN NEW YORK CITY 1785 - 1840

59 ST

B'WAY

42 ST

ST. JOHN THE EVANGELIST 1840

ST. PAUL'S HARLEM 1824

POPULATION
30, 000 → 312, 000
CATHOLICS
200 → 75, 000

ST. JOHN THE BAPTIST (GERMAN) 1840

14 ST    LINE OF SETTLEMENT

GERMAN WARDS

IRISH WARDS

ST. JOSEPH 1829

17    11

ST. NICHOLAS (GERMAN) 1833

ST. PATRICK 1809

10    13

ST. MARY 1826

TRANSFIGURATION 1836

GRAND

CANAL

5    6

ST. JAMES 1836

4

ST. PETER'S 1785

BOWERY

Church of the Most Holy Redeemer, East Third Street

Pierre Toussaint, c. 1766-1853

Pierre Toussaint's affluence was no protection against the racial prejudice that was endemic in antebellum New York. He travelled about the city each day visiting the homes of his wealthy customers. The most convenient means of transportation for him would have been the city's horsecars, but no African American was allowed to use them until the year after his death. Even in church Toussaint was not immune from offensive remarks. In the summer of 1842 he was insulted at St. Patrick's Old Cathedral by a white usher who objected to his presence. The lay president of the Cathedral's board of trustees, the French-speaking Louis Binsse, sent Toussaint an apology. In expressing his regrets, however, Binsse revealed the unconscious racism that prevailed among even the best-intentioned New Yorkers. "If God by His will has created you and your wife with black skin," said Binsse, "by His grace He has also made your heart and soul as white as snow."

Church of St. Alphonsus, Thompson Street, founded in 1847, now demolished

St. Elizabeth Ann
Seton, 1774-1821

IN MEMORY OF
ELIZABETH ANN BAYLEY SETON

The orphan asylum that was the beneficiary of Pierre Toussaint's benefactions was the first Catholic charitable institution in the city, established in 1817 by the Sisters of Charity from Emmitsburg, Maryland. The Sisters already had a connection with New York in the person of their foundress, Elizabeth Ann Seton, a widow and a former Episcopalian who was received into the Catholic Church in 1805 in St. Peter's Church on Barclay Street. She was canonized in 1975, thus becoming the first American-born saint. Bishop Connolly's invitation to the Sisters of Charity to come to New York has been described (by Monsignor Florence Cohalan) as his most important achievement. In subsequent years the Sisters of Charity were to establish their own diocesan community and to be the backbone of the parochial school system in New York.

Receipt issued to Pierre Toussaint for payment of pew rent in St. Peter's Church, February 16, 1822

31

# Lay Trusteeism

Mission of Our Lady of the Rosary, State Street, in the late nineteenth century when it served as a shelter for Irish immigrant girls

In other areas of diocesan administration Connolly found himself overwhelmed by the demands of a rapidly growing diocese with limited resources. Most of his flock were poor immigrants with little money to spare for the building of the much-needed new churches. Vocations to the priesthood were so rare that Connolly complained that "American youth have absolutely no inclination to become ecclesiastics." He was forced to rely entirely on priests from Ireland, about eighteen of whom were working in the diocese at the time of his death in 1825.

St. Mary's Church, Grand Street, New York's third oldest Catholic parish, founded in 1826

Another intractable problem that plagued Connolly throughout his episcopate was lay trusteeism, which burst into open conflict in St. Peter's Church in 1817. As in other American dioceses at that time, the quarrel was not simply between clergy and laity, but also between two rival groups of priests, with one group supporting the bishop and the other group supporting the lay trustees. Another aggravating circumstance in New York was nationalism, pitting Irish and French clergy against one another. The situation became so serious that in 1819 the trustees of St. Peter's Church sent Father William Taylor to Rome to plead their case against Bishop Connolly. (Archbishop Michael Corrigan would later call Taylor "an early example of Americanism.") The following year Rome deputed Bishop Joseph Plessis of Quebec to visit New York and conduct an investigation. Finally, in 1821 the Roman authorities banned from the diocese the three clerical ringleaders: Taylor, Malou, and Father Charles Ffrench, O.P., who was Connolly's principal supporter. At the same time Rome gave Connolly himself less than a full vote of confidence, recommending that he should ask for a coadjutor.

When Bishop Connolly died on February 6, 1825, the diocese was left unfilled for twenty-one months.

Responsibility for administering

the vacant see fell to Connolly's vicar general, Father John Power, a popular, energetic and ambitious Irish-born cleric, who had been pastor of St. Peter's Church since 1822. He displayed a tact and vision not seen in New York since the departure of Kohlmann, providing New York Catholics with their first newspaper (*The Truth Teller*), establishing a third New York City parish (St. Mary's on Grand Street) and erecting a new orphan asylum (which is still in use as the parochial school of St. Patrick's Old Cathedral). Power even managed to effect a reconciliation with Malou and to reinstate him in the ministry. New York's Irish Catholics had every reason to expect, therefore, that John Power would be their next bishop. Instead they were surprised and disappointed to discover in the fall of 1826 that their new shepherd was to be John Dubois, a native of Paris, France.

Interior of the Church of the Most Holy Redeemer

34

# Bishop
## JOHN DUBOIS

Dubois was born in Paris in 1764 and fled his native land in 1791 during the early stages of the Revolution. He landed in Virginia and lived briefly in Richmond where he was even invited to celebrate Mass for the city's tiny Catholic population in the state capitol, apparently without provoking any outcry that he was undermining the foundations of Mr. Jefferson's wall of separation between Church and State. Bishop Carroll soon appointed Dubois pastor of a parish in Frederick, Maryland, and in 1808 Dubois began another career when he founded Mount St. Mary's College and Seminary in Emmitsburg, Maryland.

Bishop John Dubois, 1764-1842

Then, at the age of sixty-two, he was appointed the third Bishop of New York and was dropped into a strange new diocese where he was made to feel unwelcome from the day of his episcopal ordination in Baltimore, October 29, 1826, when the preacher, Father William Taylor, presented a grim picture of the situation that the new bishop would find upon his arrival in New York.

Dubois tried to mollify the New York Irish by placing a shamrock on his episcopal crest and by confronting the question of nationalism directly in his first pastoral letter. "Who are those who

object to our foreign birth?" he asked. "Are they not in the same sense foreigners themselves?" He analyzed the situation correctly when he said: "The question was not why an American had not been appointed, but why was not an Irishman." Dubois offered his flock a quick lesson in Church history when he raised the question whether "the apostles (were) natives of the countries to which they were sent to preach the Gospel?" Even more pointedly, he asked: "Is St. Patrick less the patron of Ireland for having been born in Gaul?" Such arguments made little impression on priests and people

who had confidently been expecting the appointment of John Power as their next bishop. In fact, Bishop Dubois had difficulty even in communicating this pastoral letter to his people, for the editor of *The Truth Teller*, Father Thomas Levins, refused to print it in New York's only Catholic newspaper.

Dubois also inherited Connolly's problems with the lay trustees. At the new St. Joseph's Church in Greenwich Village (established in 1829), the trustees were especially assertive, so much so that the parish had four pastors in three years. Not until the appointment of young Father John McCloskey

Sanctuary of St. Mary's
Church, Grand Street

(the future Cardinal) as pastor in 1837 did the bishop feel that he was securely in control of the parish. In his own Cathedral, Dubois was often at loggerheads with the trustees. A nasty scene ensued when Dubois suspended Levins, who was a curate at the Cathedral. The trustees retaliated by hiring Levins as director of the parish school and threatening to cut off Dubois' salary. His response to their threat was a classic. "You may vote the salary or not just as seems good to you," he told them. "I am an old man and do not need much. I can live in a basement or a garret. But, whether I come up from the basement or down from the garret, I shall still be your Bishop."

In 1828 and again in 1829, in the pre-railroad era, Dubois made extensive visitations of his diocese, which still included the whole state of New York and the northern half of New Jersey. Then, from September 1829 until November 1831, Dubois was in Europe, seeking priests and money. In 1836, when requesting money from the Archbishop of Vienna, he estimated that there were 200,000 Catholics in his diocese in a general population of 2,000,000. By that time he reported that he had 33 completed churches and four oratories. In New York City alone there were six completed churches and one under construction, but he complained that "we need twelve more churches, if we had the means of building them, for more than half of the faithful hear Mass outside the vestibule." Throughout the state there were fifty private homes where Mass was regularly celebrated "because there is no other accommodation."

The presence of the Sisters of Charity was already noticeable. By 1836 they were conducting three free schools, but Dubois valued

St. Joseph's Church, Greenwich
Village, founded in 1829

36

Reverend Thomas Farrell,
Pastor of St. Joseph's
Church, 1857-1880

them even more for their work in caring for the many Catholic orphans, who almost certainly would have been lost to the faith, if they had been placed in secular institutions, which (like the public schools) were strongly Protestant in atmosphere. The Sisters of Charity operated five orphan asylums, two in New York City, and others in Brooklyn, Albany and Utica, several of which were partially funded by the government.

In New York City Dubois was responsible for the establishment of the new parishes of St. Joseph in Greenwich Village (1829), St. Paul in Harlem (1834), St. James (1836) and Transfiguration (1836). Brooklyn had received its first parish, St. James, in 1822. Outside the city Dubois also founded parishes in Saugerties (1833), Cold Spring (1834), Poughkeepsie (1836), Newburgh (1837) and New Brighton on Staten Island (1839). In 1836 he accepted into the diocese a seminarian recently arrived from Europe, ordained him a priest three weeks later, and sent him to an

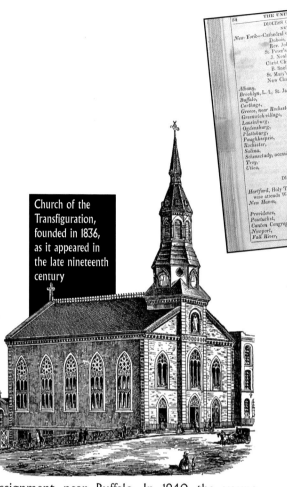

assignment near Buffalo. In 1840 the young priest left the diocese to join the Redemptorists, later became Bishop of Philadelphia, and was canonized in 1977. His name was John Neumann.

One of Dubois' fondest dreams was to supply New York with its own seminary. He purchased a 162-acre farm in Upper Nyack for such an institution in 1832 and spent every spare dollar he had on the construction of a three-story stone building over the next four years. Just as it neared completion, however, it burned to the ground as a result of an accident by a careless workman. A wealthy layman, Cornelius Heeney, offered Dubois property in Brooklyn for a seminary. However, nothing came of the proposal because Heeney had little regard for Dubois' financial acumen and refused to surrender the title to the property to him. John Power shared Heeney's reservations about Dubois' lack of administrative abilities. "The bishop will never get any (financial) help from the people," said Power, "because they have no opinion of his prudence."

**N.Y. Weekly Register, &c.**

SATURDAY, FEBRUARY 1, 1834.

CATHOLIC CHURCHES IN NEW-YORK.

*Et ait Dominus ad David \* \* \*. Quod cogitasti in corde tuo ædificare domum nomini meo, bene fecisti.*

"And the LORD said to David \* \* \* Whereas thou hast thought in thy heart to build a house to my name, thou hast done well." \* \* \*

3 *Kings* 8, 18.

The Catholics of New-York have much reason to be thankful to that Divine Providence who has ever watched over the interests of his chosen people, for the flourishing state of their religion throughout every section of this powerful Republic.

How wide the difference between the state of Catholicity at the present day in New-York, and that of fifty years ago! Then there existed not one solitary chapel, in which a few scattering members of the Catholic Church could assemble to offer up their homage to the throne of Mercy;— now there are six, frequented and supported by numerous and respectable congregations. Then there was only an occasional clergyman, who came from afar; an uncertain and precarious visitant to a cowering flock;—now there are twelve officiating clergymen, with our venerable Bishop; all constantly and zealously engaged in the onerous and awful duties of their sacred ministry.

*New York Weekly Register and Catholic Diary, February 1, 1834, reports on the progress of Catholicism in New York City*

## SACRAMENTAL LIFE IN NEW YORK IN THE 1830's

The paschal time here may be said to last throughout the year. The number of priests is not sufficient to allow them to hear a quarter of the confessions within the paschal time. Day laborers and other workmen who are mostly employed by Protestants cannot go to confession except Saturday evenings and Sunday mornings when the throng is so great that only a part can be heard. Many must wait for hours and find themselves obliged to go home without being able to approach the Sacrament of Penance. Many cannot hear Mass for months and even for years because their employers do not allow them to leave work on Sunday mornings. If, nevertheless, they leave work, they are in danger of losing their employment; if they are out of work, they must starve with wife and children. In spite of all the difficulties, the zeal of all my Catholics exceeds belief.

I myself, another salaried priest and my chaplain who receives an uncertain salary, hear three hundred confessions a week. Not a Sunday passes without giving Communion to at least a hundred faithful. The same proportion, I think, is to be found in other parishes. In the country, the scattered condition of the parishioners causes new difficulties. From eight to ten thousand children and about six hundred adults are baptized annually.

Bishop Dubois to the Archbishop of Vienna, 1836, in *Historical Records and Studies X* (1917): 124-125.

Church of Our Lady of the Rosary and Shrine of St. Elizabeth Ann Seton, State Street

Church of St. James in the late nineteenth century in the shadow of the Brooklyn Bridge

In addition to all of his other problems, Dubois also had to face a serious outburst of anti-Catholic bigotry. Such anti-Catholic feeling had been widespread in colonial America, but it had virtually disappeared during the time of the American Revolution. It now reappeared stronger than ever, fed by resentment of the large numbers of immigrants who were pouring into the port cities of America in the 1830's and 1840's. Nativist fears focused particularly on the poor Irish Catholic immigrants in such places as Boston, Philadelphia and New York.

In January 1830 a militantly anti-Catholic newspaper called *The Protestant* made its appearance in New York City. So gullible was the editor, the Reverend George Bourne, that he published several patently bigoted letters from a correspondent who used the pseudonym "Cranmer." The letter writer then took delight in revealing his true identity. He was a young Catholic priest in Philadelphia named John J. Hughes. The same coterie of bigots who were responsible for *The Protestant* also founded the New York Protestant Association in 1831 "for the express purpose of eliciting knowledge respecting the state of Popery."

The Association sponsored several debates between Protestant ministers and Catholic priests, which predictably generated more heat than light. After a minor riot on May 2, 1832, Bishop Dubois forbade further participation by his priests. The following spring there was an attempt to resume the debates through the less incendiary medium of letters published jointly in *The Protestant* and the *Truth Teller*.

— William Craig

Brownlee, minister of the Dutch Reformed Church and Bourne's successor as editor of *The Protestant,* squared off against John Power, Thomas Levins and Felix Varela (a Cuban exile and pastor of Transfiguration Church). The three priests soon broke off the exchange, however, telling Brownlee: "Your substitute for arguments are falsehood, ribald words, gross invective (and) disgusting calumny."

One of the most popular forms of anti-Catholic "literature" was tales of escaped nuns, a form of soft-core pornography that purported to reveal the sordid happenings that many Protestants suspected took place behind convent walls. The most famous example of this genre appeared in New York City in 1836, *Awful Disclosures of the Hôtel Dieu Nunnery of Montreal,* a salacious account of convent life supposedly written by an escaped nun with the improbable name of Maria Monk. The real author was a Protestant minister in New York City, the Reverend J.J. Slocum. The prestigious publishing house of Harper Brothers was eager to reap the anticipated profits but reluctant to sully the family name by placing it on the title page. They solved their dilemma by setting up a dummy firm in the name of two employees, Howe and Bates. *Awful Disclosures* was a best seller with 300,000 copies in circulation by the Civil War, the "Uncle Tom's Cabin of Know-Nothingism," as Ray Allen Billington once called it. The most effective refutation came not from Catholics, but from Colonel William L. Stone, the Protestant editor of the *New York Commercial Advertiser,* who made an inspection of the Montreal convent and pronounced the book a total fabrication.

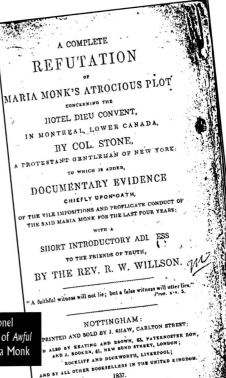

Title page of Colonel Stone's refutation of *Awful Disclosures* of Maria Monk

Archbishop
John J. Hughes,
1797-1864

## Enter John Hughes

In 1837 the aging Dubois asked for a coadjutor and received John Hughes, the Philadelphia priest who had already crossed swords with the Nativist bigots in New York. Hughes had been a priest only twelve years but was well known to Dubois. As rector of Mount St. Mary's Seminary, Dubois had initially refused to admit Hughes to the seminary because of his spotty educational background, a rebuff which Hughes never forgot. The new coadjutor was ordained in St. Patrick's Old Cathedral on January 7, 1838, the first episcopal ordination ever performed in New York.

The relationship between the two bishops was not an easy one. After Dubois had suffered a series of strokes, in August 1839 Hughes was made administrator of the diocese, to the dismay of Dubois. They lived together in the cathedral rectory for the next three years, but Dubois was virtually ignored by his coadjutor. In 1842, when Hughes dedicated the city's first French church, St. Vincent de Paul, Hughes paid tribute to a long litany of French priests who had served the Catholic Church in America. The one Frenchman whom he never mentioned was John Dubois. The old bishop died on December 20, 1842. Hughes was the preacher at Dubois' funeral and barely mentioned him even on that occasion. At Dubois' own request, he was buried under the sidewalk in front of the cathedral. Supposedly he had said: "Bury me where the people will walk over me in death as they wished to do in life."

At the death of Dubois, John Joseph Hughes immediatly succeeded him as the fourth Bishop of New York. He was to govern the New York Church for the next twenty-two years, in 1850 becoming the first Archbishop of New York. Long before that date, however, Hughes made his presence felt in America's largest city and served notice to friend and foe alike that a new day had arrived for the Catholic Church in New York.

Thomas J. Shelley

42

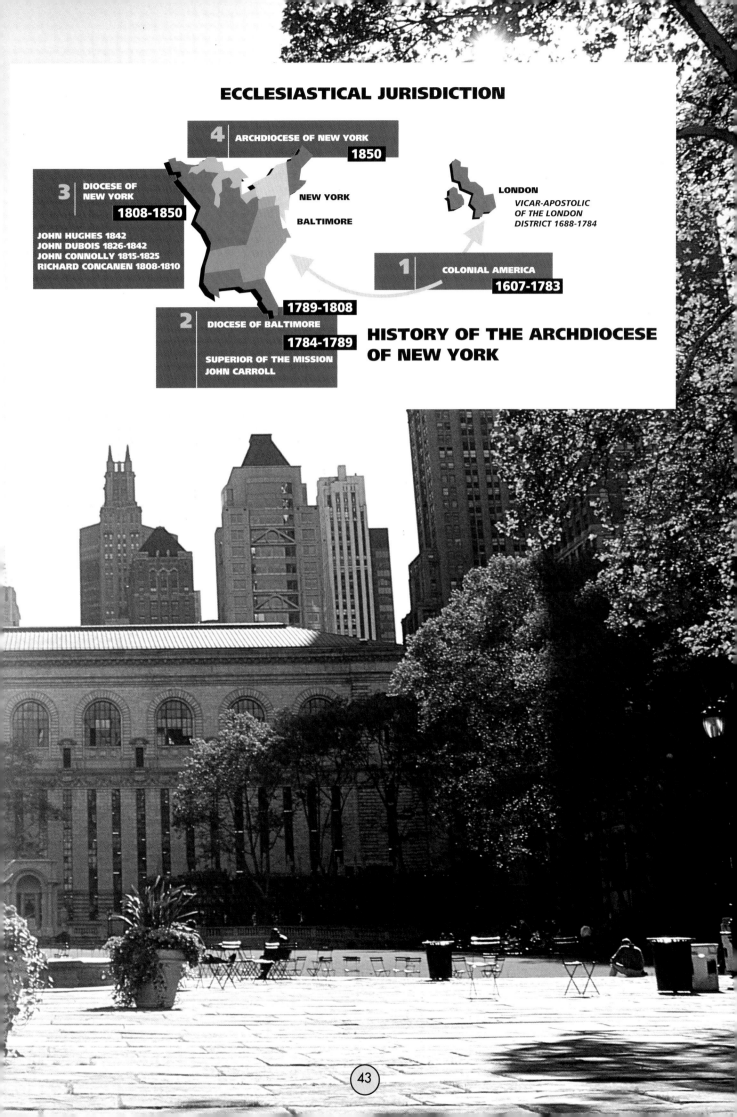

# ECCLESIASTICAL JURISDICTION

**4** ARCHDIOCESE OF NEW YORK
1850

**3** DIOCESE OF NEW YORK
1808-1850

JOHN HUGHES 1842
JOHN DUBOIS 1826-1842
JOHN CONNOLLY 1815-1825
RICHARD CONCANEN 1808-1810

NEW YORK

BALTIMORE

LONDON
*VICAR-APOSTOLIC
OF THE LONDON
DISTRICT 1688-1784*

**1** COLONIAL AMERICA
1607-1783

1789-1808

**2** DIOCESE OF BALTIMORE

1784-1789

SUPERIOR OF THE MISSION
JOHN CARROLL

## HISTORY OF THE ARCHDIOCESE OF NEW YORK

# John Hughes

## AND THE SHAPING
## OF AMERICAN CATHOLICISM

When John Hughes arrived in New York in 1838, he was an unknown quantity. By 1844 he was a national figure, one of the best known, if not exactly the best loved, Catholic prelates in the whole country. Always a fighter, Hughes stepped into three major battles during his first six years in New York. The outcome made him a national hero to many American Catholics, but also a national villain to many other Americans.

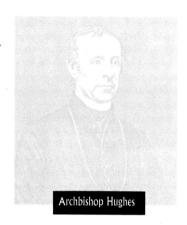

Archbishop Hughes

## The Rout of the Lay Trustees

Hughes' first battle, as was mentioned in volume one, was a continuation of the struggle between Bishop Dubois and the lay trustees of the cathedral parish. Dubois had recently suspended Father Thomas Levins from the cathedral staff whereupon the trustees promptly hired him to run the parish Sunday school. The situation got even nastier one Sunday when the trustees summoned the police to remove a Sunday school teacher appointed by Dubois. As that point John Hughes decided to act, for, he said, the civil law invoked by the trustees to remove a teacher from the classroom gave them "the same right to remove a priest from the sanctuary." With the full approval of Dubois, he decided to appeal from the trustees to all the dues-paying parishioners (the pewholders) who had elected them.

Hughes called a public meeting for Sunday, February 24, 1839. Over 600 people showed up at the meeting. They were not only the pewholders of the cathedral, but Catholics from all over the city, including trustees from other parishes. It was probably the largest meeting of Catholics in the city's history to that date. Hughes was not only a born

fighter, but also a born orator who knew how to sway a crowd, especially a crowd of Irishmen. "New York has become a bye-word of reproach to the Catholic name throughout the land," Hughes told them bluntly. He said that the dispute between Bishop Dubois and the trustees was a matter of divine law versus civil law. Then he accused the trustees of treating poor old Bishop Dubois in the same demeaning way that the British government had treated the Catholic Church in Ireland.

CHURCH OF SAINT PAUL.
EAST ONE HUNDRED AND SEVENTEENTH STREET.

The sixth-oldest parish in Manhattan, founded by Bishop Dubois in rural Harlem in 1834.

St. Patrick's Old Cathedral, the site of Bishop Hughes' confrontation with lay trusteeism in New York.

25 E 4

New York Febr. 25. 1839.

Most Rev. & Dear Sir

The battle has been fought, & the Church has triumphed. The Samson of Trusteeism has fallen without snapping a pillar, or disturbing a tile of the Sacred edifice. Te Deum laudamus — Te Dominum Confitemur.

After writing to you on monday, I got the Bishop to bind himself that he would leave me to manage the whole business, with his own authority to any extent it might require — even the closing of the Church if necessary. I then wrote the Pastoral Address which I send by this mail, and in my turn on thursday evening — the Church being crowded — I announced that at High Mass the sunday following I should publish it from the pulpit of the Cathedral — requesting the pew holders, parents and heads of families to be in attendance. Accordingly, yesterday they were in full attendance — and as many as the Church could hold of the most respectable catholics of the City. It was read slowly — and listened to with a stillness & attention the like of which I never witnessed in so large a multitude. I could read the sensation it was producing. I called them to meet at ½ past three in the vestry to root out the evils of which it complained, and establish by their own act, the true principles of their religion which it set forth. And never was call more gloriously responded to. They met at the time appointed. The vestry was too small — and we adjourned to the very school room which the rascally Constable had procured.

Bishop Hughes' letter to Archbishop Samuel Eccleston
of Baltimore, boasting of his victory over the lay trustees.
Courtesy of the Archives of the Archdiocese of Baltimore.

46

He warned them that the "sainted spirits" of their ancestors were looking down upon them from heaven and would "disavow and disown them if... they allowed pygmies among themselves to filch away rights of the Church which their glorious ancestors would not yield but with their lives to the persecuting giant of the British Empire."

Hughes claimed that, by the time he had finished speaking, many in the audience were weeping like children, and he added: "I was not far from it myself."

John Hassard, Hughes' later secretary and biographer, said that he had the crowd eating out of his hand. He could have gotten anything that he wanted from them. What he wanted and got was a resolution affirming the full rights of the bishop. With this triumph over the trustees of the cathedral, Hughes effectively destroyed lay trusteeism throughout the diocese with the notable exception of the

German national parish of St. Louis in Buffalo. The young bishop was jubilant over his victory. He boasted to Archbishop Samuel Eccleston of Baltimore that the trustees "have not strength enough to give a decent kick," and he told Bishop Joseph Rosati of St. Louis: "It is a revolution, and, I trust, a happy one in its consequences for religion." However, the thoroughness of his victory boomeranged on him to some extent, for it scared many Protestants who considered it somehow "un-American" that this Irish-born prelate should deprive the Catholic laity of any role in the governance of their Church.

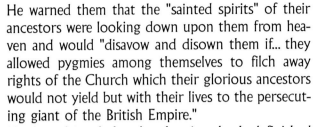

Original church of Our Lady of Loretto, Cold Spring (now a museum), 1834, the oldest Catholic church building in the Hudson Valley.

# The Public School Society

John Hughes walked into an even bigger battle in the summer of 1840 when he returned home from Europe after a nine-month begging tour trying to raise funds for a college and seminary. "The diocese was in ferment," Hughes said, and the source of the ferment was the condition of the New York City public schools. The schools were operated by a private charitable organization, the Public School Society, which was funded by the state legislature. Dominated by Presbyterians (according to Hughes), the Public School Society had turned the city's public schools into inter-denominational Protestant schools with mandatory readings from the King James version of the Bible and the daily recitation of Protestant prayers. Catholic practices such as the sacrament of penance were openly ridiculed in some of the textbooks. In fact, the whole atmosphere in the city's "public" schools was so anti-Catholic that many Catholic parents refused to send their children to these schools. As a consequence it was estimated that one-quarter of the city's children received no education at all.

Protest against the Public School Society, 1840.

St. Patrick's Church, Verplanck, the oldest parish (1843) in present-day Westchester County.

Catholics were not the only ones who were alarmed at this state of affairs. In January 1840, in his annual message to the state legislature, Governor William H. Seward, called attention to this scandal. "The children of foreigners," he said, "are too often deprived of the advantages of our system of public education in consequence of prejudice arising from differences of language or religion." In order to remedy this situation, Seward said: "I do not hesitate, therefore, to recommend the establishment of schools in which they may be instructed by teachers speaking the same language and professing the same faith..." Not unreasonably, the Catholics of New York interpreted the Governor's remarks as an invitation to ask for a share of state funds for their own schools. Catholic lay leaders in New York City formed a Catholic Association and elected Father John Power of St. Peter's church as chairman.

Church of St. Mary of the Snow, Saugerties.
When the parish was established in 1833, it was the only organized Catholic community between New York City and Albany.

This was the "ferment" that Hughes encountered upon his return from Europe in July 1840. He quickly put himself at the head of the movement. His battle with the Public School Society lasted twenty-two months, from July 1840 to April 1842, and took a heavy toll on the bishop's time and health. His friends noticed even the change in his appearance as he led the fight first before the Common Council of the City of New York and then in the state legislature in Albany. "Certainly from 1840 to 1844 he was one of the best abused men in the country," said John Hassard.

Scenes from St. Peter's Church on Staten Island. The parish was founded in 1839.

50

Interior of St. Joseph's Church, Greenwich Village, the oldest (1833) unaltered Catholic church structure in New York.

St Patrick's Old Cathedral

Hughes expected opposition from the Whigs, but he was annoyed and angry that the Democrats failed to give him any political support. Therefore, in the state elections of November 1841, Hughes did something that no other American Catholic bishop has done before or since. Four days before the election, he encouraged a group of Catholics in New York City to form their own political party, the Carroll Hall ticket. They did not expect to win the election, but to be the spoilers and to cost the Democrats the elections. The Catholic party got only 2,200 votes, but the Democrats lost New York City by a mere 290 votes. The Catholic vote may not have been decisive, but it was a warning to the Democrats not to take the Catholic vote for granted.

More than his battle with the trustees, it was Hughes' struggle with the Public School Society that made him a national and even an international figure. Ultimately Hughes destroyed the Public School Society.

USA 32 Social Reformer
Padre Félix Varela

In April 1842 the state legislature passed the McClay Bill, which replaced the Public School Society with elected school boards. However, it was a bittersweet victory for the bishop because the new law specifically forbade religious instruction in the public schools. It led eventually to the secularization of the public school system, a result which Hughes neither intended nor desired.

Moreover, Hughes outraged many American Protestants because he overturned the cozy arrangement whereby they had turned the "common schools" into Protestant public schools. They claimed that such schools were non-sectarian because they were inter-denominational and therefore eligible for government funding. By this same reasoning, however, since the Catholic Church refused to consider itself as just another denomination, Catholic schools were labeled sectarian and declared ineligible for government funding. When John Hughes challenged this double standard in New York City, he was pilloried across the country as the Catholic hierarch who wanted to drive the Bible from the public schools and finance his own schools from the public till. As a result of his conflict with the Public School Society, Hughes decided to build his own parochial school system. "The time has almost come," he said in 1850, "when we shall have to build the schoolhouse first and the church afterward."

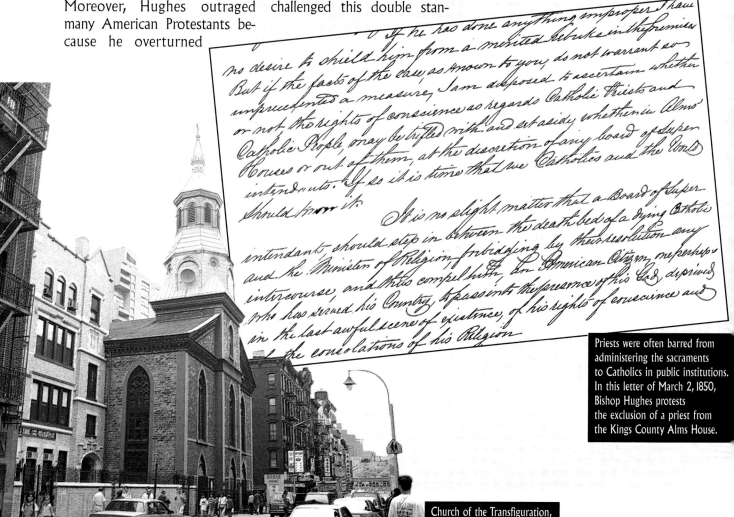

Priests were often barred from administering the sacraments to Catholics in public institutions. In this letter of March 2, 1850, Bishop Hughes protests the exclusion of a priest from the Kings County Alms House.

Church of the Transfiguration, Mott Street.

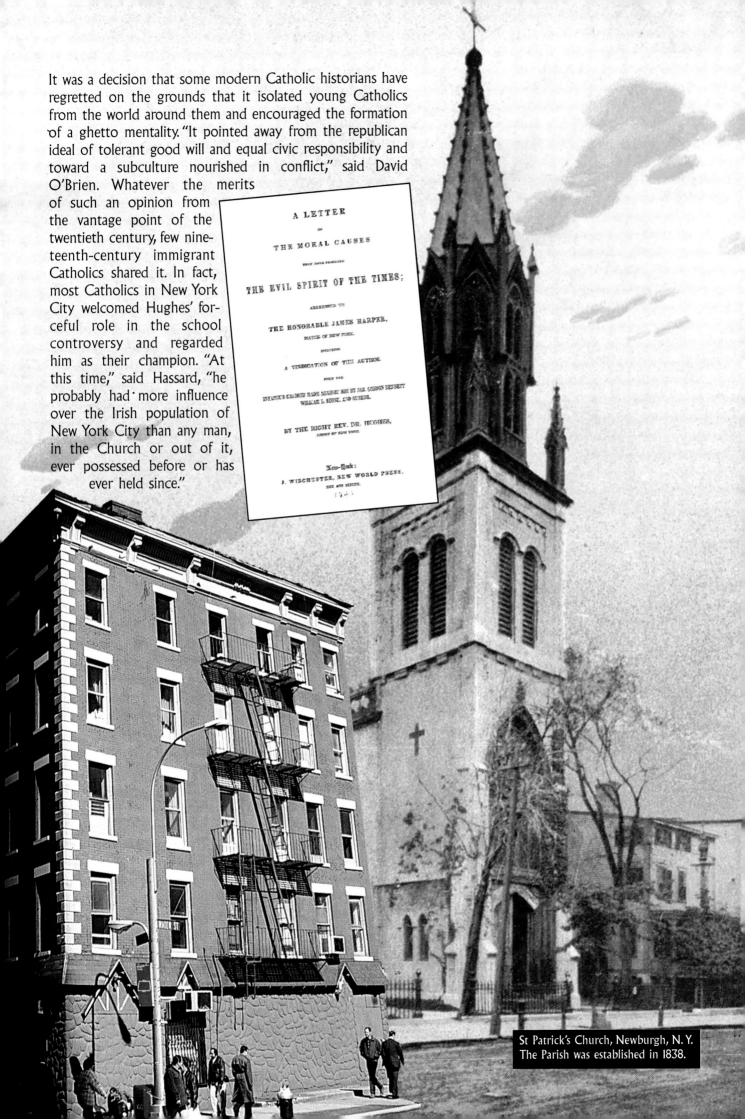

It was a decision that some modern Catholic historians have regretted on the grounds that it isolated young Catholics from the world around them and encouraged the formation of a ghetto mentality. "It pointed away from the republican ideal of tolerant good will and equal civic responsibility and toward a subculture nourished in conflict," said David O'Brien. Whatever the merits of such an opinion from the vantage point of the twentieth century, few nineteenth-century immigrant Catholics shared it. In fact, most Catholics in New York City welcomed Hughes' forceful role in the school controversy and regarded him as their champion. "At this time," said Hassard, "he probably had more influence over the Irish population of New York City than any man, in the Church or out of it, ever possessed before or has ever held since."

A LETTER
ON
THE MORAL CAUSES
THAT HAVE PRODUCED
THE EVIL SPIRIT OF THE TIMES;
ADDRESSED TO
THE HONORABLE JAMES HARPER,
MAYOR OF NEW YORK.
INCLUDING
A VINDICATION OF THE AUTHOR
FROM THE
INFAMOUS CHARGES MADE AGAINST HIM BY JAS. GORDON BENNETT
WILLIAM L. STONE, AND OTHERS.
BY THE RIGHT REV. DR. HUGHES,
BISHOP OF NEW YORK.
New-York:
J. WINCHESTER, NEW WORLD PRESS.
XXX 30TH STREET.
1844.

St Patrick's Church, Newburgh, N. Y.
The Parish was established in 1838.

# The Nativists

ot on the heels of the school controversy came another battle which showed John Hughes at his feisty best. In the 1840's the rising tide of Catholic immigrants provoked a reaction from native-born Americans who felt threatend by the influx of these newcomers. Nativist reaction was especially strong in Philadelphia and New York City both of which had large concentrations of poor Irish immigrants by the mid-1840's.

In May 1844 Nativist riots in Philadelphia led to the destruction of two Catholic churches and several dozen private residences owned by Catholics. Bishop Francis Patrick Kenrick, a shy and bookish man, left the city and ordered the suspension of Catholic religious services in order to prevent further bloodshed.

Nativist leaders in Philadelphia claimed that the Irish Catholics had desecrated an American flag. They made the flag a *cause celèbre* and announced plans to bring the flag to New York City in order to rally Nativist forces there. Preparations were made for a demonstration in City Hall Park to welcome the Nativist delegation from Philadelphia. The situation was so tense and dangerous that Hughes went to the mayor and asked him to ban the proposed

gathering. Other prominent figures did the same, and under this severe public pressure, the Nativist leaders themselves called off the demonstration.

John Hughes claimed credit for saving the city from bloodshed. Writing anonymously in the *Freeman's Journal*, he said: "There is not a [Catholic] church in the city which was not protected with an average force of one to two thousand men—-cool, collected, armed to the teeth, and with a firm determination, after taking as many lives as they could in defense of their property, to give up, if necessary, their own lives for the same cause."

There is no reason to doubt Hassard's assertion that Hughes also said that "if a single Catholic church were burned in New York, the city would become a second Moscow." One must wonder, however, to what extent Hughes' rhetoric matched reality. He may very well have posted some volunteer guards around the city's Catholic churches, but it is hard to believe that he could really have raised a private militia of 10,000 to 20,000 men without attracting the attention of either the civil authorities or the press. Nonetheless, Hughes' aggressive leadership, whether it was largely bluff or not, helped to prevent bloodshed in New York City in May 1844. Ray Allen Billington, the preeminent historian of American nativism, gave the embattled bishop high marks for his stand and credited him with "saving New York from a period of mob rule such as that which had racked Philadelphia."

# From Diocese

Roman Catholic Orphan Asylum

## TO ARCHDIOCESE

### New York Catholicism in 1839

When Bishop Hughes was made administrator of New York in 1839, the diocese had been in existence for thirty-one years, but little had been done to organize it properly. There were only 38 churches and 50 priests to care for a Catholic population of about 200,000 scattered over all of New York state and northern New Jersey. In that vast area there were only two Catholic schools and a few orphan asylums, all staffed by the Sisters of Charity of Emmitsburg, the only religious community in the diocese. There was no Catholic hospital, college or seminary. Rectories were non-existent even in the cathedral parish. "The churches were too few," said Hughes, "and these [were] in debt to an amount greater than they would have brought at public auction." He added: "The people were too poor and for a long time the increase of their numbers only added to their poverty as emigrants arrived in our port from Europe penniless and destitute." It is no wonder that Hughes confided to a friend shortly after his arrival in New York: "I feel that I have been appointed in punishment for my sins."

St Francis of Assisi
Midtown Manhattan

In 1842 the new bishop summoned the first synod in the history of the diocese to lay down basic rules for such matters as the administration of the sacraments and the ownership of church property. Henceforth, all real estate was to be vested in the bishop's name and no pastor was to spend more than $100 without his permission. One of the most urgent priorities in the diocese was the construction of more churches as the potato famine in Ireland and unsettled conditions in Germany sent several million refugees fleeing to America in the 1840's and 1850's. The plight of the Irish famine victims was especially pitiable. "The utter destitution in which they reached these shores," said Hughes, "is almost inconceivable." "The scattered debris of the Irish nation," he called them.

The number of Catholics grew so rapidly that in 1847 two new dioceses were established in upstate New York, one in Buffalo and the other in Albany. Only six years later, in 1853, two more new dioceses were established in Newark and Brooklyn for New Jersey and Long Island respectively. Not one of the four new dioceses had even three dozen priests.

In the meantime, on July 19, 1850, John Hughes became the first archbishop of New York when the diocese was made a metropolitan see. By the time of Hughes' death on January 3, 1864, the archdiocese was only one-tenth the size of the original diocese, but the Catholic population had doubled to about 400,000. New York City (then limited to Manhattan) probably had a Catholic majority by 1864. In 1861 the northern boundaries of the archdiocese were adjusted to conform to county lines and they have remained the same ever since.

St. John the Baptist, West Thirtieth Street.

New York City around 1840

# The New Metropolis

New York City underwent a major transformation during Hughes' years. In 1838, only 34,000 people lived north of 14th Street and one-third of them listed their occupation as agricultural. During the next twenty-five years, however, a whole "new city" grew up between 14th Street and 42nd Street with a population of about 190,000. The total population of the city reached almost 800,000. The growth was so rapid and so unregulated that it left New York a dirty, fetid, disease-ridden city subject to periodic outbreaks of typhoid, cholera and smallpox.

To be sure, the Croton reservoir began to supply the city with clean drinking water in 1842, but the benefits of "Croton water" were slow to materialize because, as late as 1857, three-quarters of the city's streets still had no sewers. Fewer than half of those born in New York City in the 1850's survived to the age of six. Public health actually declined in that decade. In some years deaths exceeded births. One reason for the high mortality rate among children was the prevalence of "swill milk"—milk from cows who were fed the swill or waste products of distilleries. In one notorious dairy in Williamsburg, half the cows died every year.

Living conditions aggravated the dangers to public health, especially for the poor who were packed into airless and unsanitary tenements. Such hovels constituted perfect breeding grounds for "consumption" (tuberculosis), which Bishop Hughes once called "the natural death of the Irish emigrants." Until the passage of the first tenement house law in 1867, decent lodging was frequently beyond the means of the poor. In the 1850's a common laborer earned less than $5.00 per week, but the *New York Times* estimated in 1853 that a family of four needed $12.00 per week to survive. It is little wonder that in 1858, 64% of the people admitted to the Alms House were Irish.

Church of the Immaculate Conception, East Fourteenth Street

Crime too was an ever-present menace. Walt Whitman called New York "one of the most crime-haunted and dangerous cities in Christendom" and warned visitors to avoid the streets and parks at night. The chief of police estimated in 1850 that there were 3,000 vagrant children roaming the streets. In 1851 one-quarter of the 16,000 criminals sentenced to the city prison were minors under twenty-one years of age. The diarist George Templeton Strong claimed that "no one can walk the length of Broadway without meeting some hideous troops of ragged girls, from twelve years old down, brutalized almost beyond redemption by premature vice..."

Church of the Blessed Sacrament, Upper West Side

Church of the Sacred Heart, West Fifty-First Street

The historian Edward Spann has pointed out that New York City at mid-century had also become "the capital of Protestant America," containing the headquarters of powerful inter-denominational organizations like the American Bible Society that formed the so-called Benevolent Empire. Many Protestant leaders, said Spann, "made no secret of their belief that Roman Catholicism was alien and inferior." Undeterred by either the poverty of his own people or the prejudice of others, however, there in the capital of nineteenth-century Protestant America, John Hughes set about fashioning and shaping a diocese that for the next one hundred years would be the largest and most prominent see in the American Catholic Church.

# Brick and Mortar

In 1859 Hughes said that he had dedicated 97 churches in the previous twenty years, an average of one new church every ten weeks. In the area that remained under his jurisdiction after 1853, he established 61 new parishes, 24 in New York City and 37 in the country. Among them were St. Raymond's (1842), the first parish in what later would become the Bronx; and St. Patrick's in Verplanck (1843), the first parish in present-day Westchester county. Other country parishes followed in rapid succession, generally strung out along the lines of the new railroads that radiated north and west of the city.

Isaac Hecker, founder of the Paulist Fathers

Holy Trinity Church, West Eighty-Second Str

In New York City a quarter of the new Catholic churches were purchased from Protestants, for the exodus of the middle class from lower Manhattan had begun well before the Civil War. When Catholics erected new church buildings, they almost invariably located them in the middle of the block because they could not afford to buy the more desirable corner plots. Some of the city parishes contained enormous numbers of people. Father Jeremiah Cummings, pastor of St. Stephen's church on East 28th Street, told Hughes "that about ten thousand people attend some service in the church every Sunday." In addition Cummings and one assistant priest were responsible for the pastoral care of 1,000 patients in Bellevue Hospital. In the neighboring parish of the Immaculate Conception on East 14th Street, only 6,000 of the 20,000 parishioners could find space at the five Sunday Masses, and the priests averaged ten sick calls each day.

Church of St. Paul the Apostle, West Fifty-Ninth Street

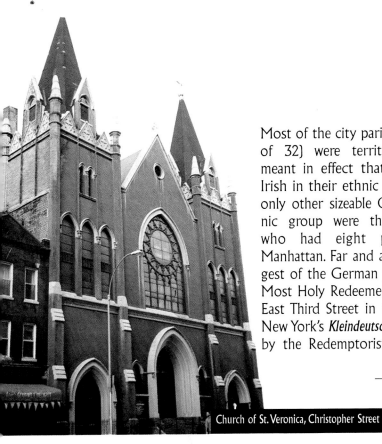

Most of the city parishes (23 out of 32) were territorial, which meant in effect that they were Irish in their ethnic makeup. The only other sizeable Catholic ethnic group were the Germans, who had eight parishes in Manhattan. Far and away the largest of the German parishes was Most Holy Redeemer located on East Third Street in the heart of New York's *Kleindeutschland*. Staffed by the Redemptorists, the huge church averaged crowds of 6,500 to 9,500 people every Sunday. Hughes took little interest in the German members of his flock perhaps because he regarded them as "exceedingly prone to divisions and strifes among themselves and with their pastors." Early on he appointed the Austrian-born Father John Raffeiner as his vicar general for the Germans and left their care largely in his hands.

Church of St. Veronica, Christopher Street

The only other national parish was the French parish of St. Vincent de Paul on West 23rd Street. Italians were still surprisingly few in New York, only about 5,000 of them by 1860. In 1857 an attempt was made to provide them with a national parish, St. Anthony of Padua, but it only lasted three years and came to an abrupt end when the pastor, Father Antonio Sanguinetti, incurred Hughes' ire by collecting money in the "Irish" parishes without his permission. There was also a small Catholic African American population, the most prominent member of which was the saintly Pierre Toussaint. Sadly Hughes took no interest in the African Americans. In fact, in 1853, the same year that Pierre Toussaint died, a black Catholic in New York, Harriet Thompson, wrote to Pope Pius IX complaining that Hughes "did not recognize the black race to be a part of his flock" and asserting that he had such a strong antipathy to blacks "that he cannot bear them to come near him."

Education was a major priority for Hughes from the day he set foot in New York. In fact, said Hassard, "the subject of all others that he had nearest his heart was education." After his battle with the Public School Society, he began to build his own parochial school system. By 1864 three-quarters of the parishes had schools, 12 of them "select" schools that charged tuition and the other 31 "free" schools. By 1870 the school buildings themselves were worth more than $2,000,000 and there were 22,125 children enrolled in them, 19% of the city's school population. Ironically, however, as Jay Dolan has pointed out, despite all of Hughes' efforts, this represented a decline of one percent from 1840 when 20% of the children had been in parochial schools. It was simply impossible to provide a Catholic education for all Catholic children.

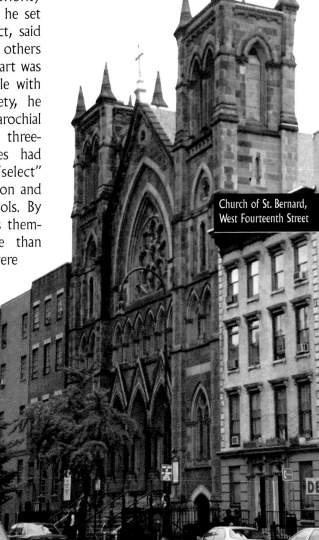

Church of St. Bernard, West Fourteenth Street

# New Religious Communities

Academy of the Sacred Heart

Catholic education in New York would never have gotten off the ground without the assistance of the religious communities of men and women. In 1838 the only religious community in the diocese was the Sisters of Charity from Emmitsburg. During the next few years, Hughes brought to New York five additional communities of women and five communities of men. In 1846 the Sisters of Charity became embroiled in a dispute with him over the staffing of the Roman Catholic Orphan Asylum, a conflict which led to a division in the community. Of the 62 sisters in New York, 29 returned to Emmitsburg while the remaining 33 sisters formed their own diocesan community, the Sisters of Charity of St. Vincent de Paul. They grew rapidly in later nineteenth century, from 33 in 1846 to 930 in 1885, providing many of the teachers for John Hughes' new parochial schools.

The Religious of the Sacred Heart came to the diocese in 1841

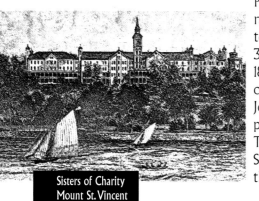
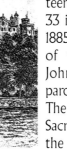

Sisters of Charity Mount St. Vincent

and opened an academy on Houston Street, which was moved in 1847 to Manhattanville. The prospectus for the academy announced that it was intended for "young ladies of the higher class." Tuition was a steep $250, but there were 264 students by 1864, an indication of a developing Catholic middle class with social aspirations for its daughters. To their credit, the sisters also used the tuition from the academy to operate a free school for the poor.

House of Mercy

Hughes was especially fond of the Sisters of Mercy whom he personally invited to the diocese on a trip to Dublin. The first seven sisters arrived from Ireland in 1846 and took over the building on Houston Street vacated by the Religious of the Sacred Heart. In 1849 they established a House of Mercy, which was both a residence and a training school for single immigrant girls. The House of Mercy was so successful that it found jobs for no fewer than 8,000 girls during its first five years of operation.

The other new women religious were the Ursulines who opened an academy in Morrisania in 1855; the School Sisters of Notre Dame who came from Germany in 1857 to staff the parochial school of Most Holy Redeemer parish and begin an German orphan asylum in Yorkville; and the Sisters of the Good Shepherd who established a home for delinquent girls on East 14th Street in 1857.

Original Motherhouse of the Sisters of Charity of St. Joseph in Emmitsburg, Maryland

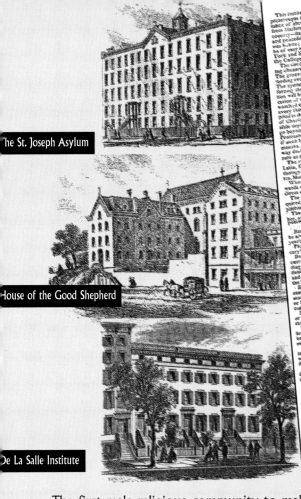

The St. Joseph Asylum

House of the Good Shepherd

De La Salle Institute

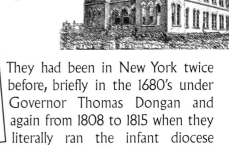

Church of St. Augustine and Church of St. Jerome, Bronx, in 1878.

The first male religious community to make a permanent foundation in New York was the Redemptorists who came to the diocese in 1842. Hughes valued their services for two reasons. They staffed several of the big German parishes such as Most Holy Redeemer, St. Alphonsus and Immaculate Conception in Melrose. They also specialized in giving parish missions in both German and English. Their preaching was very much of the fire-and-brimstone variety; one of them gave such a vivid description of hell from the pulpit one summer day when the windows of the church were open that a passerby summoned the fire department.

The Fathers of Mercy, a small French religious community, arrived around 1842 to take charge of the French parish of St. Vincent de Paul. A few years later the first Brothers of the Christian Schools also arrived from France. They provided teachers for a number of parochial schools and started an academy that eventually developed into Manhattan College.

Hughes was especially happy to have brought the Jesuits back to the diocese.

They had been in New York twice before, briefly in the 1680's under Governor Thomas Dongan and again from 1808 to 1815 when they literally ran the infant diocese under the capable leadership of Father Anthony Kohlmann. Their "Third Coming" occurred in 1846 when Hughes invited a group of exiled French Jesuits in Kentucky to take charge of his new college and seminary at Fordham. He also assigned to them the parish of St. Francis Xavier in Manhattan.

Unfortunately his relationship with them was often stormy; one fracas in 1859 was settled only when three Jesuit superiors apologized to Hughes on bended knees.

Hughes also tried to bring the Dominican friars to New York. Aware perhaps of the Jesuits' difficulties with Hughes, their Master General politely but firmly rejected the invitation. He was more successful with the Missionary Society of St. Paul the Apostle (the Paulists), the first religious community of men founded in the United States. Hughes welcomed Isaac Hecker and the other founding members of the community to the diocese in 1858. At the Church of St. Paul the Apostle, the Paulists not only established their motherhouse but also ran a large parish that was noted for the quality of its liturgy and catechetical programs.

The original Church of the Immaculate Conception, Melrose, as it appeared in the 1870s.

St. Peter, Fordham University chapel window

The first St. Joseph's Seminary, Fordham. The building was erected in 1845.

College of St. Francis Xavier,
West Sixteenth Street

## Higher Education

John Hughes' interest in Catholic education was not limited to elementary schools; he was also eager to have a Catholic college and seminary in his diocese. In 1839 and 1840 he spent nine months in Europe trying to raise funds for this purpose. Upon his return to New York in 1840 he started St. Joseph's Seminary at Fordham with twenty students and a faculty of one. The following year he opened St. John's College at the same location with a slightly larger faculty and six students. Both institutions were in the hands of the diocesan clergy, but diocesan priests were so much needed in parochial work that Hughes was happy to hand over both institutions to the Jesuits in 1846. They remained in charge of the seminary until 1855 when they withdrew after a series of disputes with Hughes. He kept the seminary open for another five years with diocesan priests, but then he was forced to close it in 1860 due to lack of money and faculty. "The pride of my early episcopacy," he called it nostalgically.

St. John's College fared better than the seminary although Hughes was not happy with the Jesuits' management of the institution. A few years after handing it over to them, he complained that it had "retrograded and become relatively obscure." Whatever the merits of Hughes' criticism, St. John's College was the first permanent Catholic college in New York and after the turn of the century it developed into Fordham University.

In 1850 the Jesuits opened another college in New York, St. Francis Xavier College, a day school which lasted only until 1911. While the tuition at St. John's College was $200 per year, at St. Francis Xavier it was only $60 per year, putting it within reach of the Catholic lower middle class. In its brief sixty-one year existence, St. Francis Xavier College easily outshone its rival at Fordham. It produced a whole phalanx of successful Catholic businessmen and professional people who for several decades constituted the lay Catholic elite in New York. Membership in its alumni association, the Xavier Union, was so coveted that it developed into the highly regarded Catholic Club of New York with over 1,000 members and a stately clubhouse on Central Park South.

The interior of the Church of St. Francis Xavier, designed by Patrick Keely, noted Irish-American church architect.

The College of St. Francis Xavier as it appeared in the City Directory of 1870.

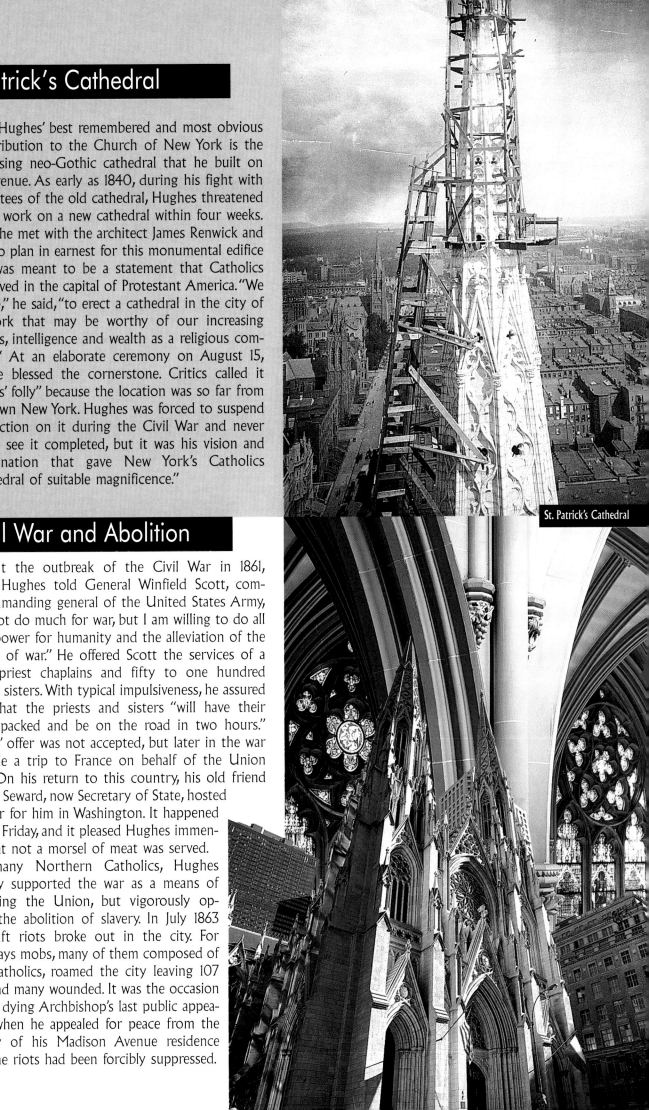

## St. Patrick's Cathedral

John Hughes' best remembered and most obvious contribution to the Church of New York is the imposing neo-Gothic cathedral that he built on Fifth Avenue. As early as 1840, during his fight with the trustees of the old cathedral, Hughes threatened to start work on a new cathedral within four weeks. In 1853 he met with the architect James Renwick and began to plan in earnest for this monumental edifice which was meant to be a statement that Catholics had arrived in the capital of Protestant America. "We propose," he said, "to erect a cathedral in the city of New York that may be worthy of our increasing numbers, intelligence and wealth as a religious community." At an elaborate ceremony on August 15, 1858, he blessed the cornerstone. Critics called it "Hughes' folly" because the location was so far from downtown New York. Hughes was forced to suspend construction on it during the Civil War and never lived to see it completed, but it was his vision and determination that gave New York's Catholics "a cathedral of suitable magnificence."

St. Patrick's Cathedral

## The Civil War and Abolition

At the outbreak of the Civil War in 1861, Hughes told General Winfield Scott, commanding general of the United States Army, "I cannot do much for war, but I am willing to do all in my power for humanity and the alleviation of the horrors of war." He offered Scott the services of a dozen priest chaplains and fifty to one hundred nursing sisters. With typical impulsiveness, he assured Scott that the priests and sisters "will have their trunks packed and be on the road in two hours." Hughes' offer was not accepted, but later in the war he made a trip to France on behalf of the Union cause. On his return to this country, his old friend William Seward, now Secretary of State, hosted a dinner for him in Washington. It happened to be a Friday, and it pleased Hughes immensely that not a morsel of meat was served.

Like many Northern Catholics, Hughes strongly supported the war as a means of preserving the Union, but vigorously opposed the abolition of slavery. In July 1863 anti-draft riots broke out in the city. For three days mobs, many of them composed of Irish Catholics, roamed the city leaving 107 dead and many wounded. It was the occasion for the dying Archbishop's last public appearance when he appealed for peace from the balcony of his Madison Avenue residence after the riots had been forcibly suppressed.

# John Hughes:
## HIS PLACE IN HISTORY

John Hughes left his mark upon New York Catholicism as no other person has done before or since. Impetuous and authoritarian, a poor administrator and worse financial manager, indifferent to the non-Irish members of his flock and prone to invent reality when it suited the purposes of his rhetoric, John Hughes nonetheless through sheer strength of character won the grudging respect of his opponents and the unconditional loyalty of the New York Irish who composed the vast majority of the local Catholic community. In addition to his native intelligence and bravery, the secret of his success is to be found in his ability to identify himself so thoroughly with the problems and difficulties of his fellow Irish immigrants. Born in County Tyrone in 1797, he once said that, for the first five days of his life, he was "on social and civil equality with the most favored subjects of the British Empire." Once he was baptized a Catholic, however, he immediately became a second-class citizen. As a young emigrant without education or skills, he spent his first few years in America as a common laborer. Thus he had firsthand experience of the prejudice and poverty that were the lot of most Irish immigrants of his day. He never forgot his roots and became a fearless and articulate spokesmen for his people. Governor Seward told him: "You have begun a great work in the elevation of the rejected immigrant, a work auspicious to the destiny of that class and still more beneficial to our common country."

He has been judged harshly by such scholars as the sociologist Andrew Greeley who wrote that "Hughes' influence can only be considered a major disaster [because of] his posture of pugnacious militancy vis-à-vis non-Catholics in American society." In fact, he could be equally pugnacious in dealing with his own clergy. When some Irish-American priests complained that he had ignored their rights in canon law, he replied that "he would teach them [County] Monaghan canon law and send them back to the bogs whence they came." "In New York no one had to ask who ruled the church," said Jay Dolan. "John Hughes was boss... He ruled like an Irish chieftain."

Like many public figures of comparable stature, Hughes will remain forever controversial as revisionist historians debate his merits and shortcomings. Perhaps John Tracy Ellis offered the most balanced view to date. Ellis deplored Hughes' bluster and lack of tact, and admitted that he was "not what one would call a likeable character." Nonetheless, Ellis insisted on the necessity of judging him in the context of his own time. Writing in 1966, Ellis reminded a Catholic critic of Hughes that "the Protestantism of the 1840s, or for that matter, the Protestantism of the United States down almost to the present decade, was in no sense the ecumenical-minded, irenic Protestantism [that]...has so radically altered its tone within regard to Catholicism in recent years..." For that reason, said Ellis, "there were times when [Hughes'] very aggressiveness was about the only approach that would serve the end that he was seeking, viz., justice for his people."

"This magnificent building was projected by the late Archbishop Hughes; the cornerstone was laid August 15, 1858. It is situated between Fifty-first and Fifty-second Streets [sic], on the east side of the Fifth Avenue, running back to Madison Avenue. The building, with its appurtenances, will occupy the entire block. The site is the most elevated on Fifth Avenue, there being a gradual descent both southerly and toward the Central Park on the north. A more eligible location could not have been chosen for so vast and imposing a structure." Manual of the Corporation of the City of New York, 1868.

# The Gilded Age

The four decades between the end of the Civil War and the beginning of the twentieth century are often called the Gilded Age in American history. It was the era when the United States became the leading industrial country in the world. As the economy boomed, a favored few made huge fortunes in railroads, mining, manufacturing, banking and related enterprises. The rich found it relatively easy to become richer in a day when there was neither a minimum wage nor an income tax nor inheritance taxes. Not surprisingly, by 1890 there were no fewer than 4,000 millionaires in the nation. Nowhere was the booming economy more noticeable than in New York City. Between 1860 and 1900 the population of the city quadrupled, from 813,000 to 3,473,000. The latter figure reflects the expanded municipal boundaries established in 1898, which now included Brooklyn, Queens and Staten Island as well as Manhattan and the Bronx.

By 1900 New York City had more people than all but six states and was home to one-quarter of the nation's millionaires. It was also the headquarters for two-thirds of the 100 largest corporations in the nation. In 1901 its factories produced more than one billion dollars worth of goods, products that ran the gamut from the clipper ships of the East River shipyards to Duncan Phyfe furniture to Henry Steinway's pianos to jewelry, clothing and even cigars.

New York City in the 1880s

Thirsty New Yorkers could take solace in the knowledge that the city's breweries produced more of the poor man's champagne than those of Chicago, Milwaukee and St. Louis combined.

On May 24, 1883, New Yorkers gathered to witness one of the great engineering marvels of the century, the opening of the Brooklyn Bridge, linking the first and third largest cities in the country.

Unfortunately, the inaugural date also happened to be Queen Victoria's birthday, a coincidence not appreciated by the city's Irish Catholics who nearly rioted to show their displeasure. Four years earlier, however, on May 25, 1879, they had had their own moment of glory, when they turned out *en masse* to take part in the dedication of St Patrick's Cathedral, a potent symbol of the Irish Catholic presence in New York.

During America's Gilded Age a favored few made huge fortunes, but many others lived in dire poverty, a contrast which was clearly evident in New York City. Fifth Avenue became known as Millionaires' Row as the Vanderbilts, Whitneys, Astors and others vied with one another in erecting impressive *faux chateaux*. A few miles away, however, on the Lower East side of Manhattan, the mansions of the wealthy gave way to grimy and unsanitary tenements. In that part of the city newly-arrived immigrants were crowded together under such appallingly inhumane conditions that the population density reached 640,000 people per square mile, a figure unmatched even in the worst slums of Calcutta. Many of the newcomers were Jews and Italians, and they kept coming in ever-increasing numbers until the eve of the First World War. In the year 1907 alone, 250,000 Jews arrived in New York from Eastern Europe; by the following year there were 500,000 Italians in New York, more Italians than there were in Rome.

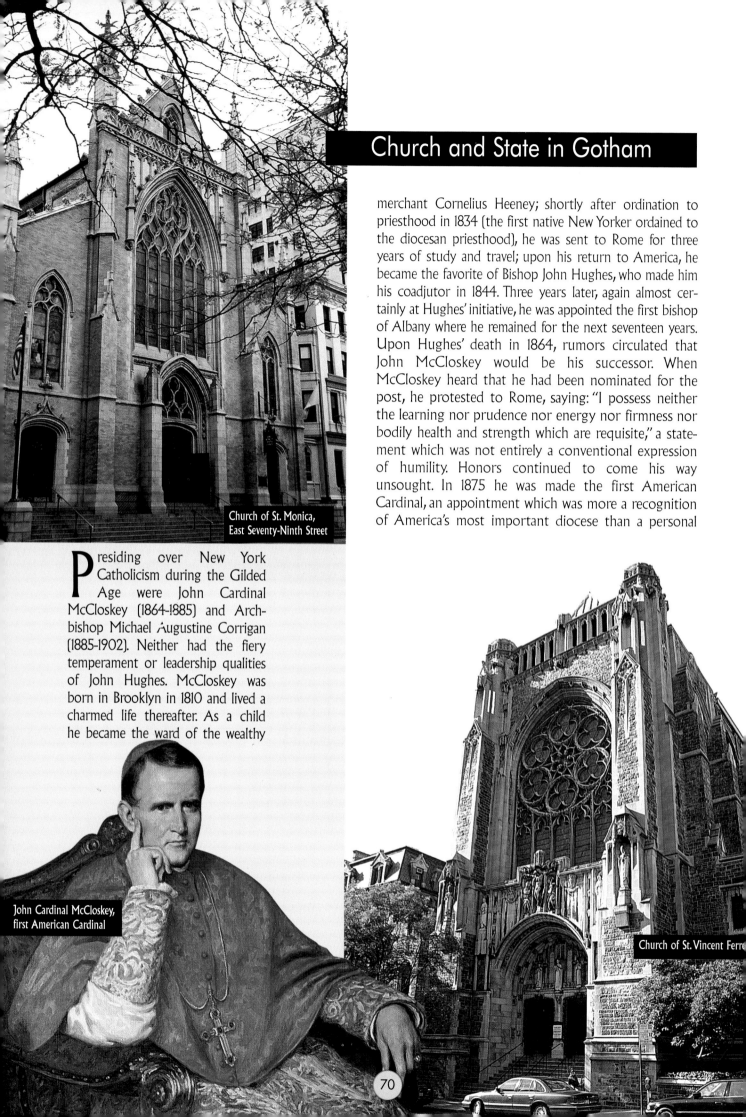

Church of St. Monica,
East Seventy-Ninth Street

P residing over New York Catholicism during the Gilded Age were John Cardinal McCloskey (1864-1885) and Archbishop Michael Augustine Corrigan (1885-1902). Neither had the fiery temperament or leadership qualities of John Hughes. McCloskey was born in Brooklyn in 1810 and lived a charmed life thereafter. As a child he became the ward of the wealthy

John Cardinal McCloskey, first American Cardinal

merchant Cornelius Heeney; shortly after ordination to priesthood in 1834 (the first native New Yorker ordained to the diocesan priesthood), he was sent to Rome for three years of study and travel; upon his return to America, he became the favorite of Bishop John Hughes, who made him his coadjutor in 1844. Three years later, again almost certainly at Hughes' initiative, he was appointed the first bishop of Albany where he remained for the next seventeen years. Upon Hughes' death in 1864, rumors circulated that John McCloskey would be his successor. When McCloskey heard that he had been nominated for the post, he protested to Rome, saying: "I possess neither the learning nor prudence nor energy nor firmness nor bodily health and strength which are requisite," a statement which was not entirely a conventional expression of humility. Honors continued to come his way unsought. In 1875 he was made the first American Cardinal, an appointment which was more a recognition of America's most important diocese than a personal

Church of St. Vincent Ferre

ch of St. Jean Baptiste

In the early 1870s, after the ouster of the notorious Boss Willam Tweed, the Irish took control of Tammany Hall, the local Democratic organization, and dominated it for most of the next century. Tweed's successor at Tammany Hall was "Honest" John Kelly, who was married to John McCloskey's niece. Kelly, the son of Irish immigrants, had a genius for organization. It was said of him that "he found Tammany a horde and left it an army." In 1880 New York Catholics demonstrated their political clout by electing the city's first Catholic mayor, William R. Grace, who quickly demonstrated his own political independence by breaking with Tammany Hall.

"By 1885," said John Talbot Smith, a New York diocesan priest and historian, "the island of Manhattan had become a Catholic city," but he groused that "this would have become more apparent but for the extreme caution of the political leaders, who feared consequences to themselves were it known." A good case in point was the composition of the Board of Education which never numbered more than two or three Catholics among its twenty-two members.

tribute to its leader. McCloskey's most impressive achievement was the completion of St. Patrick's cathedral in 1879. Aside from that important accomplishment, however, McCloskey was a person who responded to events rather than shaped them. Sometimes he did not even do that. In 1865, when two well-informed priests told him that he needed to build fifty additional churches, he rejected their advice and complained that they were exaggerating the size of the Catholic population.

During the Gilded Age no Catholic laymen in New York could rival the fortunes of the Vanderbilts or Morgans, but a few did achieve substantial wealth on a more modest scale such as banker Eugene Kelly, shipping magnate William Grace, entrepreneur Thomas Fortune Ryan and contractor John Crimmins. Many more climbed into the ranks of the middle class, while others found the road to advancement through politics. Among the latter was the endearing rascal George Washington Plunkett who held down three municipal jobs simultaneously while announcing, "The Irish was [sic] born to rule, and they're the honestest [sic] people in the world."

Father John Talbot Smith

The New York Foundling Hospital in the late Nineteenth Century.

# Charity and Social Service

In the age of laissez-faire capitalism, government did little to alleviate the sufferings of its poorest citizens. Private charity was expected to furnish whatever relief was available,

St. Vincent's Hospital in 1869

and New York's Catholics provided the city with some of its most important charitable institutions. Two of them date from John Hughes' episcopate. During the cholera epidemic of 1849, the Sisters of Charity established St. Vincent's Hospital, the first Catholic hospital in the city. The original facility, under the direction of Hughes' own sister, Sister Angela Hughes, was a rented house that lacked even running water. In 1863 John Hughes founded the Catholic Protectory, a combined orphanage and reform school for children who otherwise would have been remanded by the courts to state institutions. In 1865 it moved to bigger facilities in the Bronx on the present site of Parkchester where eventually some 3,000 youngsters were educated by the De LaSalle Brothers and the Sisters of Charity. When it finally closed its doors in 1938, the Catholic Protectory had provided custodial care for some 100,000 boys and girls.

A widespread problem in nineteenth-century urban America was in-

Levi Silliman Ives, convert Episcopalian bishop and first director of the Catholic Protectory.

The Catholic Protectory, Parkchester

fanticide and the abandonment of unwanted infants. To combat this evil in New York City, in 1869 Sister Irene Fitzgibbon, a Sister of Charity of Mount St. Vincent, founded one of the city's most famous institutions, the New York Foundling Hospital. Four years later the hospital moved to 68th Street where its red-brick Victorian buildings occupied a whole square block between Third and Lexington Avenues. In the 1890s, under Sister Irene's inspiration, the Foundling Hospital gave rise to additional specialized hospitals for children, unmarried mothers, and tuberculosis patients. When Sister Irene died in 1896, the *New York Times* praised her as "the most remarkable woman of her age in her field of philanthropy."

Another significant figure in the same field was Father John Drumgoole, a diocesan priest ordained at the age of fifty-three in 1869, the same year that Sister Irene opened her Foundling Hospital. Two years later he became director of the St. Vincent de Paul Home for Homeless Boys and spent the rest of his life caring for these street urchins many of whom made their living as newspaper pedlars.

In 1881 Drumgoole founded the Mission of the Immaculate Conception in lower Manhattan for these boys and in 1882 bought additional property on Staten Island.

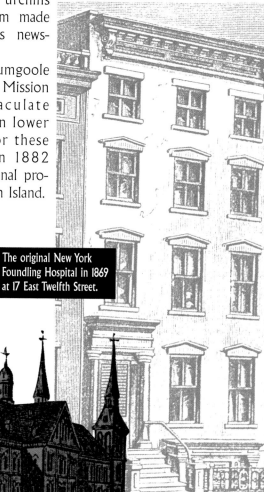

The original New York Foundling Hospital in 1869 at 17 East Twelfth Street.

St. Rose's Home, Lower Manhattan, a pioneer in hospice care

Drumgoole himself died in 1888, a victim of the great blizzard of that year. His orphanage on Staten Island for both boys and girls, popularly known as Mount Loretto, became one of the largest child-caring institutions in the country, staffed by eighty Franciscan Sisters of Hastings-on-Hudson.

Other institutions included day nurseries for working mothers, homes for working girls, Catholic immigrant agencies, hospices for terminally-ill cancer patients, and even a Fresh Air Society which sent poor city children to the country for two weeks every summer. Both St. Vincent's Hospital and Benedictine Hospital in Kingston established nursing schools. At the parish level the St. Vincent de Paul Society continued its network of activities coordinated under the direction of a devoted layman, Thomas Mulry.

At the state constitutional convention in 1894 forces hostile to the Catholic Church made a concerted effort to eliminate all state funding for religious schools or charitable institutions. The stakes were high, since the state contributed over $1,500,000 annually to maintain 20,500 residents in Catholic charitable institutions. In many ways the strife at the constitutional convention of 1894 was reminiscent of John Hughes' school controversy of fifty years' earlier with the National League for the Protection of American Interests and the Republican Party now playing the roles filled earlier by the Public School Society and the Whigs.

The Catholics responded to this challenge by executing what historian Samuel McSeveney has called "a brilliant tactical maneuver." A committee of prominent lay Catholics, headed by Judge Morgan O'Brien and working closely with the New York state bishops, decided that it was useless to try to preserve government money for parochial schools. Instead, they devoted all their effort to a campaign to maintain government funding for religious charitable institutions, an effort that ultimately succeeded thanks largely to the deft parliamentary maneuvering of two New York City lawyers, Frédéric Coudert and George Bliss.

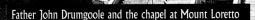

Father John Drumgoole and the chapel at Mount Loretto

Church of St. Ignatius Loyola

The first St. Joseph's Church, Yorkville, in 1878.

# Catholics and the Social Gospel

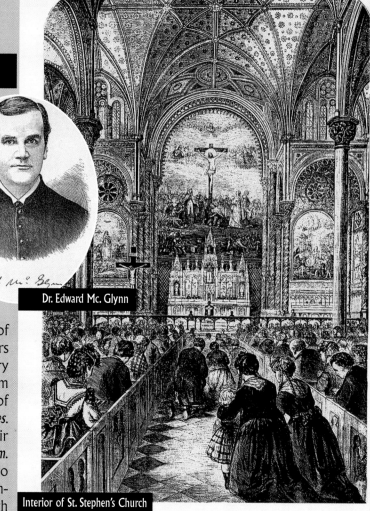

Dr. Edward Mc. Glynn

While some nineteenth-century Christians demonstrated remarkable devotion to the poor, others raised the question of why there was so much poverty in an age of affluence. These critics wished not only to alleviate the effects of poverty but also to eliminate its causes. Among American Protestants the most prominent advocate of the Social Gospel was Walter Rauschenbusch, a German-American Baptist who spent ten years working in the slums of Hell's Kitchen. In Europe prominent Catholic leaders like Bishop Wilhelm von Ketteler in Germany, Henry Cardinal Manning in England, and Frédéric Ozanam and Henri Lacordaire in France challenged many of the comfortable assumptions of the *beati possidentes*. In 1891, Pope Leo XIII would endorse much of their program in the provocative encyclical *Rerum Novarum*. In New York City the most prominent Catholic to take up the cause of social reform was the flamboyant pastor of St. Stephen's Church on East 28th Street, the Reverend Doctor Edward McGlynn. An outspoken critic of Tammany Hall and a champion of Irish Home Rule, Dr. McGlynn (as he was always called in deference to his Roman D.D.) became enamoured of the economic theories of Henry George, a social activist who advocated a single tax on land as a panacea for the inequalities in the capitalist system. In the New York City mayoral election of 1886, Henry George entered the race as the candidate of the United Labor Party, winning the endorsement of the socialists, labor unions, Irish nationalists, and reformers of every stripe, including Dr. McGlynn.

The election of 1886 set the stage for the famous confrontation between McGlynn and Archbishop Michael Corrigan, who had succeeded Cardinal McCloskey as archbishop in 1885. When McGlynn spoke at a political rally on behalf of Henry George in defiance of t.he archbishop's ban, Corrigan suspended him for two weeks. After the election Corrigan wrote a pastoral letter in defense of private property. McGlynn responded with a letter of his own to the *New York Tribune* in which he criticized "ministers of the Gospel and priests of the Church [who] tell the hard-working poor to be content with their lot and hope for good times in heaven." Further clashes led to McGlynn's removal from St. Stephen's Church and later his excommunication when he refused a summons from the pope to come to Rome.

Interior of St. Stephen's Church

"The Cross of a New Crusade": the title page of Dr. McGlynn's most famous speech

**Central Park in the Gilded Age**

The McGlynn Affair led to unprecedented discord in the New York Catholic community. From July 1887 to December 1892, McGlynn was an excommunicated cleric, but he remained popular with those New York Catholics who rightly or wrongly regarded him as a champion of the poor. As president of the Anti-Poverty Society, McGlynn retained a forum in New York and on Sunday evenings he regularly harangued his followers from the stage of the Cooper Union. Few of the New York clergy agreed with McGlynn's radical views or demagogic style, but many of them resented Corrigan's maladroit handling of the affair.

When a petition of loyalty to the archbishop was circulated among the diocesan clergy, many refused to sign it, further exacerbating the divisions in the clerical ranks. "Those who for any reason had refused to sign the address of the diocesan priests were now ranked with the opposition and were treated accordingly," said John Talbot Smith, an eyewitness of the sad events. "They were a regular opposition,"

he explained, "expecting no quarter and granting none...Thus the condition continued for many years, slowly mitigated by advance of time, but never wholly removed." Not all of the recalcitrants were motivated by affection for McGlynn. One enterprising young curate refused to sign the petition because he was unhappy with his assignment. As he correctly anticipated, the vindictive diocesan authorities promptly transferred him to another parish.

The McGlynn Affair became a national scandal and a source of embarrassment to the American bishops. Eventually Rome intervened in the person of Archbishop Francesco Satolli, who came to the United States in 1892 as a special papal envoy to the Chicago World's Fair and stayed on to become the first permanent Apostolic Delegate. In December 1892, after assuring himself that there was nothing heterodox in McGlynn's views, Satolli lifted McGlynn's excommunication. Archbishop Corrigan learned the news the next morning when he read about it in the newspapers!

# Archbishop
## MICHAEL AUGUSTINE CORRIGAN

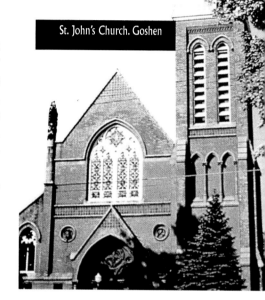
St. John's Church. Goshen

Michael Corrigan is the only Archbishop of New York in the last 100 years who failed to receive the Cardinal's red hat. A shy, pious man with an enormous appetite for paperwork, he illustrates the pitfalls of making a good executive officer the captain of his own ship. "He had a genius and love for administrative detail," said John Talbot Smith," and he added, "His chief work was the effective and minute organization of the diocese. He worked at its perfection to the last minute, and the calamities of his career never interrupted or disturbed its progress." Coadjutor to the ailing Cardinal McCloskey from 1880 to 1885, and then archbishop in his own right from 1885 to 1902, Corrigan was dogged by the fallout from the McGlynn Affair throughout his seventeen years as archbishop.

Unlike Cardinal McCloskey, Archbishop Corrigan was a national figure *malgré lui* as a leader of the conservative wing of the American hierarchy, a role which further embroiled him in controversy. He was a staunch advocate of parochial schools and won the gratitude of German-American Catholics by supporting their efforts to preserve their language and cultural heritage when "Americanist" prelates like Archbishop John Ireland of St. Paul were urging them to assimilate as quickly as possible. Unfortunately, Corrigan's sheltered youth and lack of pastoral experience left him with little awareness of the economic and social problems of most of his flock. He would have welcomed a papal condemnation of the Knights of Labor, the first large American labor union, a condemnation happily averted in 1887 by James Cardinal Gibbons with the help of Bishop Ireland and Bishop John Keane.

Controversy surrounded Corrigan not only because of his rigidly conservative views, but also because of his devious manner of promoting them. When plans got under way in 1887 for the establishment of the Catholic University of America, Corrigan was dismayed for fear that the institution, located in Cardinal Gibbons' archdiocese, would become a hotbed of liberalism. However, he came down on both sides of the issue, in America publicly supporting the establishment of the university while privately trying to undermine it through backstairs intrigue in Rome. When Bishops Keane and Ireland encountered evidence in Rome of this duplicity, they alerted their fellow bishops that "someone has been whispering against us." Their choice of verb illustrates perfectly Florence Cohalan's comment about Corrigan's "love of indirect methods [that] infuriated his opponents and bewildered his friends." Robert Emmett Curran put it more bluntly when he observed that Corrigan "seemed unable to translate private piety into public probity."

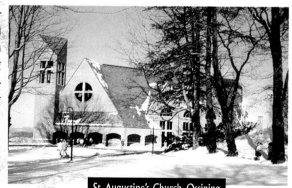
St. Augustine's Church. Ossining

Church of the Most Precious Blood, Walden

Church of St. Philip Neri
Bronx, New York

Church of the Transfiguration,
Tarrytown

Young Michael Corrigan was something of a *wunderkind* in the American Catholic Church. A member of the first class at the North American College in Rome in 1859, Corrigan became bishop of his home diocese of Newark in 1873 at the tender age of thirty-four, the youngest bishop in the United States. His predecessor, James Roosevelt Bayley, said that he had "learning enough for five bishops and sanctity for ten." In New York between 1880 and 1895, Corrigan performed all the episcopal functions in the largest archdiocese in the United States without the help of a single auxiliary bishop. It has been estimated that in those fifteen years he confirmed 194,000 people. In a pastoral letter that he issued in April 1900, Corrigan said that in the previous decade he had opened a new church, school, chapel, convent, rectory or institution every two weeks—-a total of 250 buildings. He founded ninety-nine new parishes, a record unmatched by any other archbishop of New York.

Many of the new parishes, were national parishes reflecting the influx into the archdiocese of large numbers of immigrants from Southern and Eastern Europe. This was especially noticeable in Yonkers, a Hudson River community immediately north of New York City. In the space of a few decades Yonkers was transformed from a bucolic suburb to a bustling industrial city of smokestacks and steeples whose ethnic diversity made it a small-scale replica of Pittsburgh or Chicago. In 1890 there were only two parishes in Yonkers. By 1914 there were 15 parishes of which nine were territorial and six were "national," two of them Italian, one

Church of the Immaculate Conception in Yonkers

Sanctuary of the Church of the Most Holy Trinity, Yonkers

Church of St. Casimir, Yonkers

Slovak, one Polish, one Ruthenian and one Ukrainian with smaller communities of Hungarians and Lithuanians. Archbishop Corrigan directed this massive expansion of diocesan facilities with dispatch and efficiency. However, as Marvin O'Connell points out, Corrigan was never as comfortable with people as he was with blueprints and balance sheets. Moreover, O'Connell shrewdly observes, "To a degree Corrigan's rapid climb up the greasy pole of ecclesiastical preferment had done him a disservice: he had never spent a day as a parish priest, and the common touch, that indefinable sense of the aspirations of others, was entirely foreign to him."

## Diocesan Visitation.

1883.

| | | | |
|---|---|---|---|
| Sunday, | Aug. 12. | Immaculate Conception, St. Joseph's Church, | Yonkers. " |
| Monday, | " 13. | Immaculate Conception, St. Teresa's, | Irvington. Tarrytown. |
| Tuesday, | " 14. | Our Lady of Loretto, | Cold Spring. |
| Wednesday, | " 15. | St. Francis of Assisi, St. Joseph's, | Mount Kisco. Croton Falls. |
| Thursday, | " 16. | St. Lawrence's, | Brewsters. |
| Friday | " 17. | Immaculate Conception, | Amenia. |
| Saturday, | " 18. | St. Jacob's, | Mount Vernon. |
| Sunday, | " 19. | St. Mary's, | Port Richmond : Blessing Corner Stone. |
| Monday, | " 20. | St. Peter's, St. Joseph's, | New Brighton. Rossville. |
| Wednesday, | " 22. | St. Joseph's, Immaculate Conception, | Tremont. Melrose. |
| Thursday, | " 23. | St. Joachim's, | Matteawan. |
| Friday, | " 24. | St. James', Milton, and Ireland Corners. | |
| Saturday, | " 25. | Church of the Nativity, | Poughkeepsie. |
| Sunday, | " 26. | Regina Coeli, | Hyde Park. |
| Sunday, | Sept. 2. | Blessing Chapel, Mount Loretto, Staten Island. | |
| Monday, | " 3. | St. John's, St. Catherine's, | Piermont. Blauveltsville. |
| Tuesday, | " 4. | St. Rose of Lima, | Suffern. |
| Wednesday, | " 5. | Holy Cross, | Callicoon. |
| Thursday, | " 6. | St. Mary's, | Obernburg. |
| Friday, | " 7. | Immaculate Conception, | Port Jervis. |
| Saturday, | " 8. | St. Peter's | Monticello. |
| Sunday, | " 9. | St. Joseph's, | Middletown. |
| Monday, | " 10. | Holy Name of Mary, | Montgomery. |
| Friday, | " 14. | St. Stanislaus', Polish Church. Sts. Cyril and Methodius, Bohemian Church. | |
| Saturday, | " 15. | Sacred Heart, | High Bridge. |
| Sunday, | " 16. | Dedication Church, | Dobb's Ferry. |

The Calendar of a busy Coadjutor-Archbishop. Archbishop Corrigan's schedule for five weeks in August and September 1883.

# Archbishop Corrigan and his Clergy

One reason that the McGlynn Affair caused such turmoil in the archdiocese was that Dr. McGlynn was not a lone ranger. He was part of a loosely organized group of priests who called themselves the Accademia because many of them had received part of their seminary education in Rome. Far from turning them into enthusiastic ultramontanes, however, their Roman experience left these New York priests with a decidedly unfavorable impression of European Catholicism. They returned to the United States convinced that the Catholic Church had much to gain and little to fear from a dialogue with American culture and society.

Monsignor Richard Lalor Burtsell

The godfather of the Accademia was Father Thomas Farrell, pastor of St. Joseph's Church in Greenwich Village, who was Irish born and American educated. Farrell hosted the gatherings of the Accademia at his rectory where the participants discussed such controversial topics as the Bible and evolution, papal infallibility, clerical celibacy, general absolution, vernacular liturgy and the relevance of old-fashioned religious orders to the modern world. Farrell himself incurred the wrath of the diocesan authorities when he suggested that the pope should surrender his sovereignty over the Papal States and concentrate on his role as a spiritual leader. Farrell was also one of that rare breed of Catholic abolitionists and an outspoken champion of African Americans. Indeed, Bishop John McGill of Richmond complained to Cardinal McCloskey that Farrell was guilty of "negrophily"—love of blacks—as if it were a vice or disease.

Monsignor Patrick McSweeny

At his death Farrell left $5,000 in bonds to establish a parish for African Americans in New York City. Knowing McCloskey's lack of enthusiasm for such a project, Farrell specified in his will that, if the legacy was not used for that purpose within three years, it should go to a non-Catholic charity. After waiting the full three years, McCloskey swallowed hard and used the money to establish the parish of St. Benedict the Moor in Greenwich Village. A key figure in the creation of this parish was another member of the Accademia, Father Richard Lalor Burtsell, the founding pastor of the Church of the Epiphany. A self-taught canon lawyer ("the one species of cleric so dreaded by

St. Stephen's Church,
New York
July 18 / 53.

Your Eminence,

On Friday next, the 20th inst., will be the third anniversary of the death of Rev. Thomas Farrell. In his will, which was admitted to probate and of which I am one of the executors, he left Alabama State bonds for the amount of five thousand dollars to aid in the purchase or erection of a church for Colored Catholics in this city, and he also provided that, if within three years from the time of his death no steps should have been taken by the Arch-bishop and the clergy towards the purchase or erection of such church, then the bequest should go to a certain charitable institution for colored people, which, it should be remarked, is not under Catholic control.

I write, not so much as an executor, whose strict legal duty in the matter was fulfilled by

Letter of Dr. Edward McGlynn to Cardinal McCloskey, reminding the Cardinal that nothing had been done to erect a church for African Americans in New York City.

Father John Burke and Father Augustus Tolton,
St. Benedict the Moor Church, New York City, 1886.

Cardinal McCloskey," according to John Talbot Smith), Burtsell remained a firm friend of McGlynn throughout his difficulties with Corrigan. As was probably inevitable, Burtsell too clashed with Corrigan, who removed him as pastor of Epiphany parish and exiled him to a parish in Rondout. One measure of Burtsell's stature is that he left behind a diary of over 5,000 pages which is a unique source of information for the history of New York Catholicism between the Civil War and World War I. Although Burtsell was instrumental in establishing the parish of St. Benedict the Moor, the real founder was Burtsell's curate, Father John Burke, who served as pastor from 1887 until his death in 1925. Burke also established an orphanage for African American children, St. Benedict's Home in Rye, New York. One of his proudest moments occurred in 1886 when Father Augustus Tolton, the first full-blooded black priest in the United States, came to

celebrate Mass in his church.

Still another member of the Accademia was Father Patrick McSweeny, a witty and independent-minded man of whom it was said that "nothing on this side of the grave had any terrors for him." As pastor of St. Peter's church in Poughkeepsie, McSweeny worked out an ingenious arrangement with the local school board in 1873 that came to be called the Poughkeepsie Plan. He rented his two parochial school buildings to the local school board for $1.00 per year. From 9 a.m to noon, and from 1:30 p.m. to 3:00 p.m., the two schools were "public" schools, teaching only secular subjects and were financed entirely by the local school board. Before and after regular schools hours, and at lunchtime, however, the schools were Catholic schools, with a full program of religious instruction. The arrangement, which would be the delight of many a financially hard-pressed pastor today, lasted for twenty-five years under both McSweeny and his successor, Father James Nilan, another member of the Accademia. It came to an end in 1898 when it was declared unconstitutional because of the religious habits worn by the Sisters of Charity.

Throughout his seventeen years as archbishop, Corrigan regarded the members of the Accademia (and any priest associated with them) with deep suspicion. He was encouraged in this attitude by his vicar general, the ultra-conservative Monsignor Thomas Preston, a convert Episcopalian clergyman whom historian Richard Purcell once characterized as "rather more Catholic than the pope." "It is really high time that this circle of Liberalists should receive a proper discipline,"

Preston advised Corrigan. "New York leads the country and Liberalism should be put down here," he added for good measure. With Preston's suspicions feeding his own, Corrigan made little effort to establish any rapport with the members of the Accademia, who were some of his most talented clergy. Instead, said Marvin O'Connell, "he displayed a weakness—-not unique to him by any means—-of surrounding himself with second-rate functionaries who could pose no threat to him." After most members of the Accademia had been assigned to upstate parishes far from New York City, one bemused cleric commented: "The brains of the diocese is up the Hudson!"

# MERRY CHRISTMAS ❋

## AND

## ❋ HAPPY NEW YEAR

### —TO—

## ST. BRIGID'S CONGREGATION.

· · · · · · · · · · · · · · · ·

DEARLY BELOVED IN CHRIST :

For His love and honor I beseech you to

## EXCLUDE INTOXICATING DRINKS

from your tables. or at least to have non-intoxicating beverages such as coffee, tea or soda water, side by side with them, so as to diminish as much as possible *the frightful excesses* which are incidental to this Holy Season.

Above all things

## DO NOT URGE

anyone to partake of intoxicating drink. I am fully aware that the great majority condemn the vice of Intemperance as much as I do. and it is not for any fault which I find with you that I thus address you ; but in order that you may set an *edifying example* to those who need it. Do not coöperate in the

## SLIGHTEST DEGREE

with those who outrage our Lord and His Holy Church by gluttony.

PATRICK F. MCSWEENY,

*Rector St. Brigid's*

NEW YORK CITY,
Christmas, 1887.

Archbishop Corrigan and the Italian Immigrants

One area where Corrigan satisfied even his sharpest critics was his pastoral care of Italian immigrants, who only started to come to the United States in large numbers just at the time that Corrigan took over the reins in New York. As late as 1880 there were no more than 20,000 Italians in New York City, most of them from Northern Italy. Thereafter, however, the trickle turned into a flood. Between 1880 and 1914, over 3,000,000 Italians entered the United States through Castle Garden and Ellis Island, and many of them settled permanently in the New York area.

The Italian immigrants posed special problems for the American bishops. Even the term "Italian" was something of a misnomer, for Italy had only recently been unified politically, and many immigrants thought of themselves primarily as Neapolitans or Sicilians or Milanese rather than as Italians. Many were illiterate and spoke only their local dialect which was incomprehensible to other Italians.

Italian piety also presented a stark contrast to that of the Irish, creating a cultural gulf which often left Italian parishioners and Irish-American clergy engaged in a dialogue of the deaf. The Italian immigrants' *religion folklorique*, which centered around the annual *festa* of the patron saint of their native village, seemed little better than superstition to phlegmatic Celtic clerics. On the other hand, to Italian immigrants, the silent thirty-minute Latin Mass that was commonplace in American parishes seemed more like low-church Protestantism than the Catholicism with which they were familiar in their native land. A New York pastor, Bernard Lynch, admitted in 1888 that "the Catholic Church in America is to the mass of the Italians almost like a new religion." Religious sensibilities varied even among the Italians themselves. When a priest from Tuscany was assigned to a Sicilian parish in Chicago, he asked, "Can these people be Italians?"

As far back as 1866 the Franciscans had established the first permanent Italian national parish in New York City, St. Anthony of Padua on Sullivan Street, but it soon proved inadequate to care for the needs of the growing number of Italian immigrants. In 1883, Corrigan's vicar general (and eventual successor), John Murphy Farley, told him: "Something more must be done for these poor unfortunate people." A year later Corrigan himself estimated that there were 50,000 Italians in the

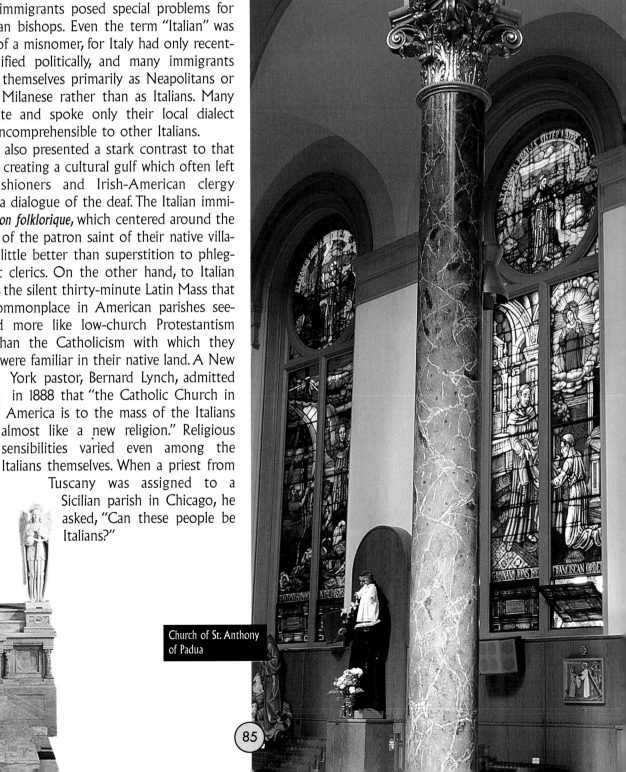

Church of St. Anthony of Padua

city, but only 1,200 of them attended Sunday Mass. He had at his disposal twelve expatriate Italian priests, but ten of them were fugitives from justice in Italy, and the people understandably shunned them. Corrigan's solution was to invite Italian-speaking religious order priests to New York. At first they served in "annexed parishes," which were often the basement churches

St. Anthony of Padua

of existing parishes such as St. Brigid's and Transfiguration. Before long they began to establish their own Italian national parishes, and Little Italy and Italian Harlem were soon dotted with Italian parishes founded and administered by the Salesians, Scalabrinians, Pallotines, Franciscans and Jesuits.

New York's Irish-American diocesan clergy also made a substantial contribution to the pastoral care of the Italian immigrants. In a Pastoral Letter

that he issued in 1889, Corrigan listed thirty-three Italian-speaking priests with names like Flynn, McManus and McSweeny. Some of them showed admirable sensitivity to the Italian immigrants. One of them, Father Patrick J. Mahoney of St. Jerome's parish in the Bronx, explained in 1893 why the Italians contributed so little to the financial support of their parishes. "*Andare alla chiesa e pagare* [Go to church and pay]," he said, "is something very harsh to a poor Italian. They have been brought up in Italy where they had to pay little or nothing." However, Mahoney, predicted that, if the Irish-American clergy treated "the present generation generously," their children and grandchildren would become the backbone of the Church in New York, a prediction that proved to be remarkably accurate. At the time of Corrigan's death in 1902 there were twenty-five Italian national and "annexed" parishes caring for over 133,000 people. According to historian Stephen DiGiovanni, the leading expert in this field, "Corrigan did his utmost, outstripping all other American bishops in his efforts in favor of the Catholic Italian immigrants."

The most famous of all Italian immigrants to America, Mother Frances Xavier Cabrini, arrived in New York City in 1889. Her initial meeting with Corrigan was not a happy one. He told her to go back to Italy in the mistaken belief that she had come to America in defiance of his orders. Once the initial misunderstanding was resolved, however, the two got on well together. Mother Cabrini personally took charge of the faltering Columbus Hospital and put it on a firm financial footing. Her Missionary Sisters of the Sacred Heart soon became familiar figures in the New York Italian community as nurses, teachers and social workers visiting poor Italian immigrants in their own homes.

**Michele Agostino Corrigan,**

DELLA SANTITÀ DI N. S. LEONE PP. XIII.,

Prelato Domestico ed Assistente al Soglio Pontificio

PER LA GRAZIA DI DIO E DELLA SEDE APOSTOLICA.

ARCIVESCOVO DI NUOVA YORK.

*Ai Cattolici Italiani dimoranti in questa Diocesi:*

CARISSIMI FIGLIUOLI, SALUTE E BENEDIZIONE:

I nobili sentimenti di paterno affetto e pastorale sollecitudine che riscaldano il petto del gran Leone XIII. verso il gregge intero della Chiesa a Lui affidato, non potevano non manifestarsi in una maniera specialissima in pro di quegli Italiani, che dando un addio o per alcun tempo o per sempre al patrio suolo, si recano a queste Americhe nella speranza di ritrovarvi miglior fortuna. Egli stesso Italiano, anzi il primo fra gl'Italiani, non potea dimenticare quei suoi connazionali, che credi d'altronde di tutte le vere glorie d'Italia, seco portavano in terra straniera quella che dirsi deve la più splendente e preziosa, cioè a dire l'unità della fede Cattolica.

Or perchè questa particolarmente, dalla quale dipende l'eterna salvezza, non abbia a patir detrimento nell'animo degli Italiani che approdano a queste spiagge, il Santo Padre Leone XIII. s'è degnato di dirigere a tutti gli Arcivescovi e Vescovi d'America in data del 10 Dicembre, 1888, una lettera piena di affetto e di sollecitudine. E giacchè questa lettera vi tocca, carissimi figliuoli, sì davvicino, stimiamo bene di farvela conoscere direttamente, nella quale vedrete

Pastoral Letter of Archbishop Corrigan to the Italian Catholics of New York, January 15, 1889

## A New Seminary

One of Corrigan's first priorities upon becoming the Archbishop of New York in 1885 was to replace the antiquated St. Joseph's Provincial Seminary in Troy, New York. He first announced plans for a new St. Joseph's Seminary at the synod of 1886. However, four years elapsed before he found a suitable site, Valentine Hill in the Dunwoodie section of Yonkers where he purchased fifty-six acres of prime real estate for $70,694.06 on March 6, 1890. The cornerstone was blessed on Pentecost Sunday, May 17, 1891, at a chaotic ceremony which drew some 60,000 people to Yonkers from New York City and left many thousands more stranded along the way. The problem was the single-track railroad line from New York City to Yonkers which could not cope with the mass of humanity who tried to make their way to Dunwoodie on that beautiful spring day. Even Archbishop Corrigan and his entourage had to abandon their stalled train and

St. Joseph's Provincial Seminary, Troy, New York, which served as New York's diocesan seminary, 1864-1896.

walk the last few miles to Valentine Hill.

It required five more years to erect the massive stone seminary building. Money was a constant problem. The architect, William Schickel, originally estimated the cost at $400,000, but his final bill was $857,627.38. Corrigan himself contributed $50,000 for the chapel, but he received no other single contribution larger than $10,000. Most of the money came in the form of small donations collected in the parish churches. By contrast, in those same years, J. Pierpont Morgan pledged $500,000 for the construction of the new Episcopal cathedral of St. John the Divine.

On August 12, 1896, the new St. Joseph's Seminary was formally dedicated by the outgoing Apostolic Delegate, Francesco Cardinal Satolli. There was still a mortgage of $250,000 on the building, but that was paid off by May 1898 as a present to Corrigan on the occcasion of his episcopal silver jubilee.

Bishop Bernard McQuaid pronounced Dunwoodie "the finest seminary building in Christendom." Even Dr. Burtsell was impressed, describing it as "a splendid building with every comfort and convenience." Perhaps the tribute that meant the most to Archbishop Corrigan was the one that he received from James Cardinal Gibbons of Baltimore, who told him: "It is no disparagement to your active and fruitful ministry to say that this is your grand crowning work and the one that will bring you the greatest consolation." Over the next century Dunwoodie would train over 2,200 priests for the Archdiocese of New York, amply repaying Archbishop Corrigan for the time and effort that he had expended on it.

THE LIGHT OF THE WORLD

IN MEMORY OF
THE MOST REVEREND
MICHAEL AUGUSTINE CORRIGAN, D.D.
THIRD ARCHBISHOP OF NEW YORK
FOUNDER OF
ST JOSEPH'S SEMINARY

# Fin-de-Siècle

At the dedication of the new seminary at Dunwoodie, Bishop Bernard McQuaid of Rochester mentioned in the presence of Archbishop Corrigan that he had been baptized (in 1823) by New York's first [resident] bishop, confirmed by the second, ordained a priest by the third, and ordained a bishop by the fourth. The septuagarian McQuaid would outlive his protégé Corrigan and live on well into the episcopacy of Corrigan's successor, John Murphy Farley.

McQuaid's lifetime spanned the era from the digging of the Erie Canal to the eve of World War I, from the presidency of James Monroe to that of William Howard Taft, a period in which the Catholic community in New York state grew from six churches and eight priests to an archdiocese of over 1,000,000 Catholics with six suffragan sees. By the 1890s rumors were already rife that Rome was contemplating a division of the Archdiocese of New York, which was the largest in population in the United States and reputedly the wealthiest.

Bishop McQuaid was exceptional but not unique in having witnessed eight decades of remarkable growth in New York Catholicism. The doughty old prelate lived on until 1909, long enough to take part during the previous year in the celebration of the centenary of the diocese. Like many other New York Catholics on that occasion, Bishop McQuaid must have wondered how his hopes for the future would measure up against the achievements of the past.

# The Begining
## OF THE AMERICAN CENTURY

### The Centennial of the Diocese

For Americans the twentieth century began in 1898 with an easy victory in "the splendid little war" with Spain and the emergence of their country as a world power. A decade later, in 1908, the Holy See finally recognized this fact and formally acknowledged that the United States was no longer a missionary country by removing it from the jurisdiction of the Congregation de Propaganda Fide. That same year the Catholics of New York had their own reasons for celebrating as they observed the 100th anniversary of the establishment of the diocese of New York. A week-long series of ceremonies began with a solemn high Mass in every parish on Sunday, April 26. The observance of the centenary was officially a religious event, but inevitably it was also a demonstration of Catholic power in New York City, especially a demonstration of Irish Catholic power.

John Cardinal Farley

The reviewing stand in front of St. Patrick's Cathedral for the parade to celebrate the centenary of the diocese, May 2, 1908.

# THE DIVISIONS OF THE ORIGINAL DIOCESE OF NEW YORK

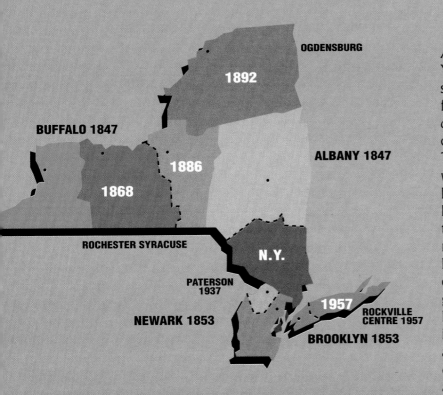

OGDENSBURG

1892

BUFFALO 1847

1886

ALBANY 1847

1868

ROCHESTER SYRACUSE

N.Y.

PATERSON
1937

NEWARK 1853

1957

ROCKVILLE
CENTRE 1957

BROOKLYN 1853

Cardinal Logue, Archbishop of Armagh and Primate of All Ireland, arrives in New York, escorted by Archbishop Farley, April 27, 1908

Although 42 of the 136 parishes in New York City were national parishes, representing eleven different ethnic groups, few would have suspected the ethnic diversity of New York Catholicism from observing the centenary celebrations. The tone was set on Monday, April 27, when Michael Cardinal Logue, archbishop of Armagh and primate of All Ireland, arrived from the Emerald Isle on the R.M.S. *Lucania*. At 6:00 a.m. that morning a delegation of 400, headed by Archbishop Farley, left the Battery on a chartered steamboat, the *Isabel*, to greet the Irish Cardinal in the lower harbor. Unfortunately the *Isabel* soon ran into a thick fogbank which immobilzed all shipping in the port for most of the day. Hours later, the *Isabel* finally inched alongside the big Cunard liner out in the Atlantic off Sandy Hook, and the diminutive Irish Cardinal appeared on deck. It was the signal for the band on board the *Isabel* to strike up a rousing rendition of *The Wearing of the Green*. Cardinal Logue was safely transferred to the *Isabel*, but it was 5:00 p.m. by the time that he reached his destination, the pier on the North River at West 50th Street. As he stepped on shore in that pre-skyscraper era, one of the first sights that he saw in the distance was a huge American flag suspended between the twin spires of St. Patrick's Cathedral. The rest of the week was filled with special events that included three pontifical Masses in as many days in the cathedral, a rally in Carnegie Hall, and a private reception for the visiting dignitaries at the Catholic Club. The grand finale took place on the following Saturday with a march of 40,000 men up Fifth Avenue past the cathedral where they were reviewed by Archbishop Farley and his guests from a special grandstand erected on the front steps. The police, largely Irish themselves of course, generously estimated that as many as 500,000 people watched the parade.

Cardinal Logue and Cardinal Gibbons enter the cathedral for the centennial celebrations of the diocese in 1908

Throughout the week Farley was the proud host, boasting that the tiny diocese of 1808 had now become an ecclesiastical province which throughout New York State contained 1,546 churches, 2,710 priests, 583 parochial schools with 251,383 students, and over 3,000,000 faithful. The center of attention, however, was not Farley, but Logue, who was lionized wherever he appeared and was invariably introduced as the "the 114th successor of St. Patrick." The Irish Cardinal responded graciously to the attention that he received, telling his American audiences that he had witnessed many processions in Rome and the Catholic countries of Europe, but never had he seen so many men publicly demonstrate their commitment to the Catholic faith. "You real [sic] young men might live to see another centennial in New York," Logue said with obvious exaggeration. "If you do," he predicted, "you will live to see the Church in New York and America the most flourishing in Christendom."

Also in attendance at most of the festivities was the sole American Cardinal, James Gibbons of Baltimore, who delivered the most memorable address of the week when he extolled the unique American heritage of religious freedom in a pluralistic society. Only nine years earlier, in a famous public letter addressed to him, Pope Leo XIII had warned American Catholics of possible dangers to their faith in the American system of separation of church and state. At that time, Cardinal Gibbons had reassured the pope that, on the contrary, Catholicism flourished in the free soil of America.

He repeated that message before a packed house in Carnegie Hall on May 1. "Let us never forget, my dear friends," he said, "to whom we are indebted under God for the blessings that we enjoy. We owe it to our country, we owe it to the freedom which we possess to think." Turning to Cardinal Logue, Gibbons added, "Here, I say, we enjoy liberty without license, Your Eminence, and authority without despotism."

Gibbons related the story of how, on his return from Vatican Council I in 1870, he had stayed at the splendid palace of a French bishop.

The French prelate said to him: "Monseigneur, all is not gold that glitters. I can't build as much as a sacristy without receiving permission from the central authorities in Paris." "Here, my dear friends," continued Gibbons, hammering home his point, "it is quite different. Here a bishop and the clergy have direct spontaneous relations with the people. That is the secret of our success."

It was vintage Gibbons, and a classic exposition of the Maryland Catholic tradition of religious freedom that would finally win the endorsement of the universal Church at Vatican Council II. It is no wonder that two days later the *New York Times* commented: "We have long believed that there was no better American than Cardinal Gibbons."

# Modernism and Dunwoodie

The one disquieting note in the centenary celebration was sounded by Archbishop John J. Glennon of St. Louis, preaching at Vespers on April 28 in St. Patrick's Cathedral in the presence of the Apostolic Delegate, Archbishop Diomede Falconio. Glennon called attention to the recent encyclical of Pope Pius X, *Pascendi Dominici Gregis*, which was a strongly-worded condemnation of a new heresy called Modernism, which the Pope described as "the synthesis of all heresies." The objective of the new heresy, the Holy Father said, was to leave "nothing stable, nothing immutable in the Church." The background to *Pascendi* was the intellectual ferment that had been taking place in the Catholic

world during the previous thirty years. Catholic scholars, encouraged by Pope Leo XIII, had been employing recent advances in history, archaeology, philosophy, literary criticism and other secular disciplines to elucidate their understanding of theology and the Bible. The results were mixed. According to Canon Roger Aubert, the famed Belgian church historian, some developments were unobjectionable and caused no controversy at all; other developments were basically sound but frightened people because of their novelty; still other developments became so radical that they were plainly incompatible with Christian orthodoxy.

Maryknoll Seminary

Maryknoll Seminary, Ossining, New York. The founding of Maryknoll, the Catholic Foreign Missionary Society of America, in 1911 was one of the signs of the coming of age of American Catholicism

*Pascendi* was aimed at this third kind of Modernism, especially as it undermined belief in divine revelation, the divinity of Christ and the definitive character of the Church's most solemn doctrinal pronouncements.

Unfortunately, however, *Pascendi* was implemented in such a heavy-handed fashion that all three varieties of Modernism were equated with the last kind and tarred with the same brush of heterodoxy. This Integralist Reaction, as the campaign against Modernism was called, degenerated into a witch hunt, and "Modernist" became a term of abuse used by ideologues as recklessly as the names "fascist" and "communist" were used at the height of the Cold War. Devout Catholics like the French Dominican exegete Marie-Joseph Lagrange, and even the young Angelo Roncalli, the future Pope John XXIII, were lumped together indiscriminately with the excommunicated French priest and scripture scholar, Alfred Loisy, one of the few genuinely heterodox Modernists.

The Integralist Reaction was largely a European phenomenon, but one of the few places in the United States affected by it was Archbishop Farley's own diocesan seminary at Dunwoodie. In the twelve years since its founding in 1896, Dunwoodie had become one of the rare Catholic intellectual centers in the United States, second in importance only to the Catholic University of America, in the judgment of John Tracy Ellis.

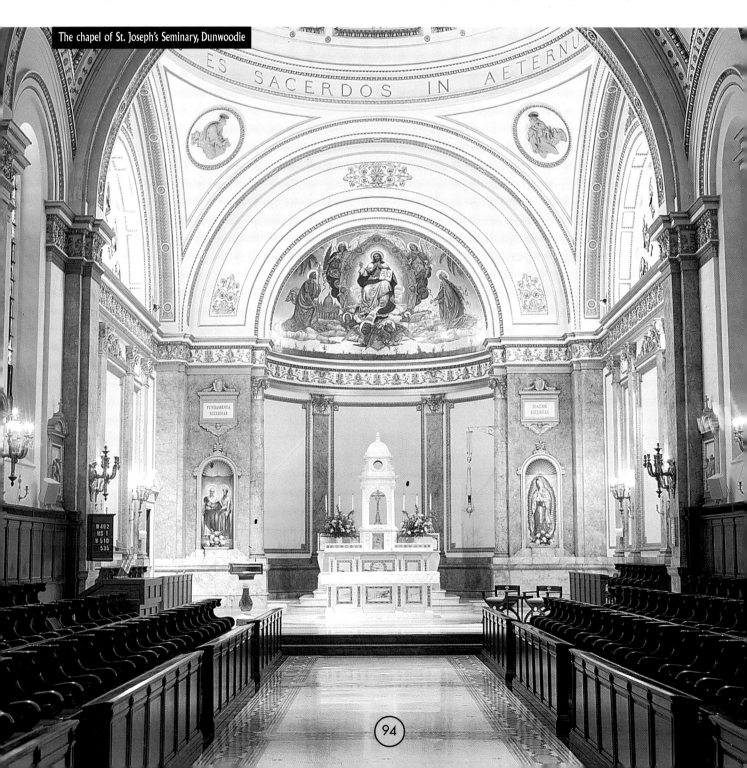

The chapel of St. Joseph's Seminary, Dunwoodie

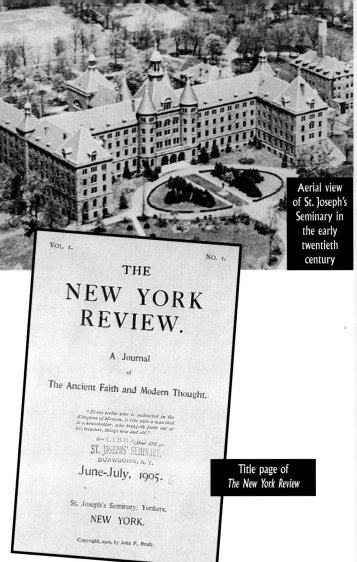

Aerial view of St. Joseph's Seminary in the early twentieth century

Title page of *The New York Review*

Driscoll was warned by Dunwoodie's first rector, Edward Dyer, that he would get little support from Farley "if a whisper of disapprobation is wafted from Rome." "[Farley] would never allow his seminary to be suspected of unsound doctrine," Dyer explained to his own Sulpician superior in Paris. "He would like to be a cardinal."

In June 1908 *The New York Review* ceased publication; in September 1909 Driscoll was forced to resign and was replaced as rector by John P. Chidwick, a hero of the Spanish-American War and chaplain of the New York City Police Department; two years later Farley was made a Cardinal. Father Joseph H. McMahon, pastor of Our Lady of Lourdes Church, predicted that, as a result of what he considered a mistaken interpretation of *Pascendi*, many Catholics "would become fearful of all progress [and] indeed become obscurantists." That was the situation which prevailed after 1908 at Dunwoodie where academic life settled into a mind-numbing routine of memorizing Latin textbooks, a form of education that historian Peter Guilday once characterized from personal experience elsewhere as "an intellectual coma."

By 1908 the Dunwoodie faculty could boast of outstanding scholars like the rector, James Driscoll, Gabriel Oussani, Francis Gigot and Francis P. Duffy, the last of whom who would later win fame as a chaplain during World War I. With Farley's blessing, in 1905 Driscoll and Duffy had founded *The New York Review,* a professional theological journal which quickly won acclaim as the best Catholic periodical of its type in the United States. The editors clearly indicated the purpose of their enterprise with the motto that appeared on the masthead of every issue, "A Journal of the Ancient Faith and Modern Thought."

In the wake of *Pascendi*, however, it became increasingly difficult to achieve this reconciliation of the ancient faith and modern thought as the influence of the integralist *zelanti* grew ever stronger. "Nothing so violent and drastic...has appeared since the days of the Inquisition," said Driscoll. "I can compare the crisis to nothing but a cyclone during which people must simply make for the cellar." Even a person of stronger character than Archbishop Farley would have found it difficult to withstand the storm when Dunwoodie came under suspicion of Modernism in Rome.

The Reverend James F. Driscoll, rector of St. Joseph's Seminary, 1902-1909

# John Murphy Farley

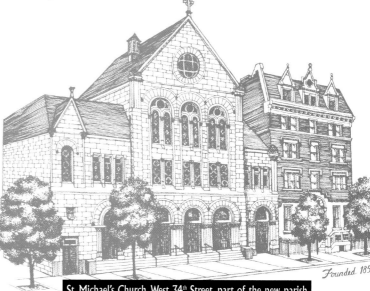

John Murphy Farley (or Farrelly as he spelled his name for the first thirty years) was the last foreign-born archbishop of New York, a native of County Armagh, where he was born on August 20, 1842. Ordained in Rome in 1870, he became New York's first auxiliary bishop in 1895, and in 1902, at the age of sixty, he succeeded his sixty-three year old predecessor, Michael Augustine Corrigan. A proverbially non-committal man even by slippery Irish standards, Farley illustrated his penchant for nailing his colors firmly to the fence during the McGlynn Affair. When the controversial petition of loyalty to Archbishop Corrigan was circulated among the diocesan clergy, Farley delayed his decision until the last minute, then added his signature to the printed list of names, thereby hoping to keep a foot in both camps.

Farley's long experience as a diocesan official convinced him of the need to unify a clergy and laity still polarized by what his vicar general, Michael J. Lavelle, referred to delicately as "the troubles of 1886 and thereafter." The new archbishop signaled his desire to heal old wounds by obtaining the title of Monsignor for two of Archbishop Corrigan's principal foes, Richard Burtsell and Patrick McSweeny. So unprecedentedly lavish was his bestowal of Roman honors (eight honorary prelates at one clip) that John Talbot Smith, who was not one of the recipients, commented impishly that the new archbishop had made half the clergy purple and the other half blue. At Farley's death, however, Lavelle mentioned as one of his principal accomplishments that "there [was] not a faction or a clique he left behind."

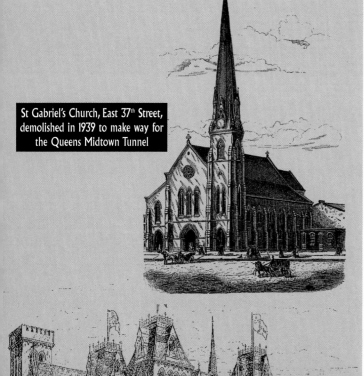

St Gabriel's Church, East 37th Street, demolished in 1939 to make way for the Queens Midtown Tunnel

St. Michael's Church, West 34th Street, part of the new parish plant built by the Pennsylvania Railroad in 1907 to replace the original buildings at a cost of $1,000,000

The Catholic population of the archdiocese grew only slightly during Farley's sixteen years as archbishop (1902-1918), from about 1,200,000 to about 1,325,000, reflecting the exodus of more prosperous Catholics to suburbs outside the archdiocese. "Brooklyn and [New] Jersey have taken away our industrious middle class," complained Father James McGean, the pastor of St. Peter's on Barclay Street, as far back as 1898. At that time, Farley, then the vicar general, advocated selling surplus downtown churches in order to pay off the debt on the cathedral and the seminary, advice which he did not follow when he became the archbishop.

The original St. Michael's Church and School on Ninth Avenue between 31st and 32nd Streets, demolished to provide the Pennsylvania Railroad with access to Penn Station

Night view of St. Raymond's Church, the oldest (1842) parish in the Bronx

The original Cathedral College, at Madison Avenue and 51st Street, opened in 1903

Two areas of the archdiocese that experienced impressive growth in the early decades of the twentieth century were the Bronx and Staten Island. Almost every year a new parish was opened in the Bronx, bringing the total to 41 by 1920 while the archdiocese registered its greatest proportional gain in Staten Island where the number of parishes jumped from 8 to 17. In Westchester too the number of parishes almost doubled, from 31 to 57. Many of the new residents of both the Bronx and Staten Island were Italian immigrants, who numbered over 400,000 throughout the archdiocese by 1918. Like Archbishop Corrigan, Farley took an active interest in their spiritual welfare, increasing the number of Italian national parishes from 18 in 1903 to 44 in 1918. Unlike Corrigan, however, who favored religious order priests from Italy, Farley preferred to staff these parishes with his own diocesan clergy. When he discovered in 1916 that there were only three Italian-American seminarians in Dunwoodie, he ordered a stepped-up campaign for vocations in the Italian parishes.

Except for the shortage of Italian-speaking priests, Farley was the first archbishop of New York who did not have to worry about vocations. "Thank God," he said in 1917, "we in this diocese have nothing to complain of." One reason for his good fortune was the effectiveness of Cathedral College, the minor seminary planned by Corrigan and opened by Farley in 1903. It was a daring innovation in seminary education, a day school consisting of four years of high school and the first two years of college.

The modern Church of St. Joseph-St Thomas, Staten Island

Before long Cathedral College was supplying Dunwoodie with 50 applicants each year, 350 of whom had been ordained for the archdiocese of New York by the time that Cathedral College celebrated its twenty-fifth anniversary in 1928.

Catholic education made impressive gains in other areas as well. Fifty new parochial schools were established during Farley's administration, doubling the enrollment on the elementary level. Catholic higher education also registered notable advances. St. John's College became Fordham University in 1904, and three women's colleges were founded in the early twentieth century: the College of New Rochelle (1904), the College of Mount St. Vincent (1910) and Manhattanville College of the Sacred Heart (1917). Manhattan College had already received its permanent charter in 1891 and moved to its present campus in Riverdale in 1923,

A major preoccupation for Farley between 1910 and 1916 was a series of city and state investigations of Catholic charitable institutions that generated considerable bad publicity such as the lurid newspaper headline: "Pigs and Children Fed from the Same Bowl." Except for his vigorous criticism of these investigations, which he regarded as an effort to undermine public subsidies to private charitable institutions, Farley kept a low public profile. Indirectly, however, he exercised considerable political clout.

The archbishop's residence at 452 Madison Avenue was widely known as The Powerhouse because of the deference paid to the archbishop by local politicians. For example, in 1904, the newly-elected mayor, George McClellan, who was not a Catholic, called upon Farley to ask if he had any Catholic candidates for city commissioners. Farley won high praise from McClellan as "a very broad-minded, liberal, fine old man" when he replied: "I should much prefer that you appoint fair-minded Protestants. All that the Church wants ... is a square deal." When Farley returned to New York from Rome with the Cardinal's red hat in 1912, the city's Protestant and Jewish leaders honored him at a dinner in the Waldorf-Astoria, an event which President William Howard Taft hailed as "an indication of the great progress we have made in mutual toleration and brotherly cooperation."

Graduation Day at Fordham University on the front steps of Keating Hall

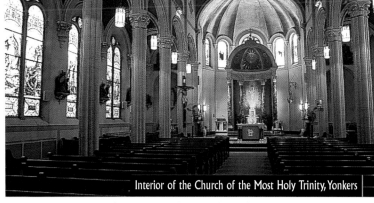

Interior of the Church of the Most Holy Trinity, Yonkers

Church of the Most Holy Trinity, Yonkers

Farley's last four years as archbishop coincided with World War I. When the United States entered the conflict in April 1917, it touched off all across the country a tremendous outburst of emotional patriotism, which most American Catholics fully shared. "We have never been wanting in any crisis in our history," said Farley, pledging his full support for the war effort. However, he did not go quite as far as William Cardinal O'Connell of Boston who announced solemnly that "the spirit of God is working through Woodrow Wilson."

The rapid expansion in the size of the armed forces created an urgent demand for Catholic chaplains whose numbers swelled from 28 to 1,525 at the war's end. The Holy See moved quickly to provide for the needs of Catholic servicemen and their families by creating a new non-territorial diocese called the Military Ordinariate with its headquarters in New York City. Heading this new diocese with the title of Military Vicar was Patrick J. Hayes, auxiliary bishop of New York and close confidant of Farley.

Of the 87 New York priests who served in World War I, far and away the most famous was Francis P. Duffy, chaplain to the New York Sixty-Ninth Infantry Regiment, which was made up largely of young Irish-Americans from New York City. Despite chronically poor health, Duffy at the age of forty-six volunteered for service with the regiment in France where he won lasting fame for his bravery under fire and dedication to his men. His commanding officer, Brigadier General Michael Lenihan, said, "I regard him as the outstanding figure of the Rainbow Division. He was first of all a priest." Honored by both the French and American governments, but never by his own Church perhaps because of the lingering taint of Modernism, Duffy's war record as a chaplain shows how unfair it was to equate his progressive theological views with heterodoxy. After the war, Duffy returned to Dunwoodie to give a lecture to the seminarians on his wartime experiences. The house historian noted in the record of the event next to Duffy's name: "He used to be a professor." It was a comment that Duffy would have appreciated.

One of Duffy's proudest moments as a chaplain occurred one day when he was standing next to some French Army officers as a detachment of American troops marched passed them. "But you know them all," the French officers exclaimed, "and they all know you, and they seem so pleased to see you."

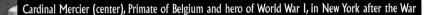

Cardinal Mercier (center), Primate of Belgium and hero of World War I, in New York after the War

As Duffy told the story later, he admitted, "I am afraid that I did not disclaim knowing all of them individually, but I did explain that the smiles that wreathed their countenances were a tribute to my priesthood rather than my person.... And that's the way I like it best."

One of the clearest indications of Catholic patriotism in World War I was the series of fund-raising drives conducted in the spring of 1918 by the National Catholic War Council, the newly established national organization of the United States bishops. Nowhere were the results more spectacular than in New York. Farley hoped to collect $2,500,000. Instead, he received $4,962,424.85, with a quarter of the total coming from non-Catholic contributors. It was the first really professional fundraising drive conducted by the archdiocese with 37,610 volunteer workers engaged in the campaign. The final sum collected was the equivalent of $6.50 from every Catholic. The lay chairman of the drive, John C. Agar, said proudly: "No campaign waged in New York has gone so far over the top as has the New York Catholic War Fund."

Father Duffy and Cardinal Hayes

# "Normalcy"

## AND THE GREAT DEPRESSION

The United States retreated from the world scene after involvement in World War I, refusing to join the League of Nations. Isolationism in foreign policy was matched by nostalgia at home for the restoration of a simpler past that had never really existed, a mythical, self-reliant America of small towns and family farms untroubled by class or racial conflict. This romanticized vision of the past had an ugly side to it, however, for its model was a white Protestant America with little room for Catholics, Jews or African Americans. In fact, all members of religious or racial minorities were likely to be identified as foreigners and lumped together with the anarchists or the boatload of alleged Bolsheviks whom Attorney General A. Mitchell Palmer dispatched to Russia with much fanfare in the fall of 1919.

In short, the Roaring Twenties was not only the decade of the flapper and the flivver, but also the occasion for one of the worst outbursts of xenophobia in American history. The immigration laws of 1921 and 1924, severely limited immigration from southern and eastern Europe. The Eighteenth Amendment, which aimed at eliminating the vices of the big cities by imposing prohibition on the whole nation, was, in the words of Sydney Ahlstrom, "the great Protestant crusade of the twentieth century." By the mid-twenties the revived Ku Klux Klan was a powerful political force in many southern and western states, and so powerful nationally that the Democratic Party convention, meeting in New York City in 1924, refused to censure the Klan. In Oregon in 1922 the voters approved a law, later declared unconstitutional by the U.S. Supreme Court, that would have forced parents to send their children only to public schools.

The decade ended with an ugly outburst of anti-Catholic bigotry during the presidential campaign of 1928 directed at the first Catholic candidate for President, Governor Alfred E. Smith of New York Most

Big-City Catholicism: the Eucharistic Congress in Chicago in 1926

American Catholics were not directly affected by this wave of bigotry. It was largely a rural phenomenon, and most American Catholics lived in the big cities of the northeast and midwest. In fact, the inter-war years were the golden age of the big city Catholic parishes. Pastors boasted of the size of their "parish plant," meaning a sprawling assemblage of buildings—church, school, rectory, convent and parish hall—that might occupy a whole square block in a solidly Catholic area of Boston, Philadelphia or Chicago. Even Protestants and Jews in those cities sometimes identified their neighborhood by the name of the local Catholic parish.

Cardinals Mundelein and Hayes outside The Powerhouse, 452 Madison Avenue

# Patrick Cardinal Hayes

Cardinal Hayes, President Eamon De Valera of the Irish Free State and Archbishop Daniel Mannix of Melbourne, Australia

Almost to the end of the inter-war period New York remained the largest of these big-city American archdioceses, presided over by Patrick J. Hayes a popular native son born on the Lower East Side of Manhattan not far from the birthplace of his near contemporary Alfred E. Smith. The son of working-class Irish immigrants (his father was a longshoreman), Hayes' childhood experience of poverty left him with a lifelong sensitivity to the social problems of his age. After ordination in 1892 and a further two years of study at the Catholic University of America, young Father Hayes was assigned to the Manhattan parish of St. Gabriel where he made a favorable impression on the pastor, John Murphy Farley. Thereafter the careers of the two men were closely intertwined with Hayes following in the footsteps of Farley as auxiliary bishop until finally succeeding him as the fifth archbishop of New York on March 10, 1919. The Cardinal's red hat followed on March 24, 1924.

During Farley's administration, the growth of the Catholic population had already leveled off, and during the Hayes' years as archbishop (1919-1938), it actually declined for the first time in history, from about 1,325,000 to about 1,000,000. As a result, in 1936 Boston supplanted New York as the largest American see. The demographic decline was due not only to the flight to the suburbs, but also due to the new immigration laws and the decline in the birthrate during the Great Depression. Nonetheless, the infrastructure of the archdiocese continued to expand. Farley established 71 new parishes, and Hayes almost matched that figure with 65 more parishes, all but five of them established before the crash of 1929. Hayes also continued Farley's practice

Catholic political power in New York: Governor Al Smith and Tammany Leader Charles Murphy

of appointing priests to an apprenticeship as rural or suburban pastors before entrusting them with a city parish.

One of Hayes' first priorities as archbishop was to address the problems in Catholic charitable institutions that had come to light as a result of the recent city and state investigations. The underlying difficulty was the lack of uniform standards in an age when poor relief was undergoing a major transformation from volunteer charitable work to professional social service. Hayes recognized the need for the archdiocese to adopt rigorous professional standards for its own charitable activities, if they were to continue to receive government funding. The stakes were high, since New York City had the largest concentration of poor and needy Catholics in the entire country.

Hayes began in 1919 with a thorough survey of the 200 separate institutions and agencies that constituted the Catholic charitable network in the archdiocese. He then organized them into the largest private charity in the United States under the aegis of a central coordinating agency, the Catholic Charities of the Archdiocese of New York, earning for himself the accolade of "the Cardinal of Charities." The key figure in establishing Catholic Charities was a young priest, Robert Keegan, a graduate of both the Catholic University of America and the New York School of Social Work.

Return of Cardinal Hayes from Rome as Cardinal in 1924

Monsignor Robert Keegan, Executive Secretary of Catholic Charities, 1920-1947

Patrick Cardinal Hayes

Church of St. Vincent Ferrer

Church of St. Vincent Ferrer

Keegan later served as the executive secretary of the organization from 1920 to 1947, making it a model for other dioceses and earning the respect of social welfare administrators throughout the country. He himself was elected president of the prestigious National Conference of Social Work in 1936, and, at the time of his death, one official of that organization commented: "Under the auspices of his diocese, [Keegan] developed the social work program of Catholic Charities until its standards were second to none in that city."

Keegan was also a notoriously irascible character whose rages were legendary. One of his assistants, Fr. Edward Roberts Moore, said that when Keegan lost his temper, which was a daily if not hourly occurrence, "all the neighbors and the neighbors' children took to the bomb shelters." Each weekday morning when Keegan left the rectory of Blessed Sacrament Church (where he was pastor) for the Catholic Charities office, a distance of several miles, the sole elevator in the office building was held at the ground floor until his arrival.

The best known priest in New York City and perhaps in the entire country, as a result of his service in World War I, was Father Francis P. Duffy, now pastor of Holy Cross Church on West Forty Second Street. His parish boundaries included both the theatre district and a swath of Hell's Kitchen, a decaying immigrant neighborhood of old-law tenements. Duffy was at home in both worlds, moving effortlessly between the *literati* and the longshoremen, and throughout the city at large. Alexander Wolcott, the literary critic, said that when Father Duffy "walked down the street—any street—he was a *curé* striding through his own village. Everyone knew him." "I had never seen so many pleased faces," said Wolcott. "Father Duffy was of such dimensions that he made New York into a small town."

It was only natural, therefore, that Alfred E. Smith, then governor of New York, would turn to Duffy for help when he came under attack because of his religion during the early stages of the presidential campaign of 1928. The occasion was an erudite article in the April 1927 issue of the *Atlantic Monthly*.

Cardinal Hayes and Governor Al Smith

The author, a distinguished Episcopalian layman, Charles C. Marshall, contended that a conscientious Catholic President could not uphold the constitution of the United States. He cited as his evidence an array of quotations from papal encyclicals that asserted the superiority of the church over the state. When Smith was first confronted with the article, he supposedly asked: "What the hell is an encyclical?"

However, the article was too important to ignore, and so Smith asked Duffy for his help in composing an answer. The result was an article in the May issue of the *Atlantic Monthly* entitled "Catholic and Patriot: Governor Smith Replies." The words were Smith's, but the ideas were Duffy's. Smith assured Marshall that the union of church and state enshrined in traditional Catholic theology applied only to totally Catholic countries, and that such countries no longer existed anywhere in the world. Smith's *pièce de résistance* was his "creed as an American Catholic," nine short, crisp sentences in which he professed his commitment to "absolute freedom of conscience for all men" and "absolute separation of church and state."

Smith's response was such a crushing refutation of Marshall that some critics accused Marshall of collusion with Smith. One friend told Marshall, "I am sure that you are destined to go down in history as the man who elected Al." For Duffy, it was a double triumph. Not only did he score a victory over bigots like Marshall, but he also had the opportunity to refute reactionary Catholic theologians whose anachronistic views gave credence to the allegations of critics like Marshall. "I have held very ardent convictions on these matters since I was nineteen years of age," Duffy confided to a friend, "and it was a matter of keen joy to me … to win a victory over the opposing Catholic school of thought." "We are Catholics and we are Americans," he added, "and to both loyalties we stick."

Hayes sent a copy of Smith's article to John Cardinal Bonzano, the former Apostolic Delegate to the United States, who was then a cardinal in the Roman curia. Bonzano pronounced Smith's article a *"capo lavoro"*—"a masterpiece," and he added, "it was judged such by everyone here who knows conditions in America." Duffy showed commendable courage in expressing his forthright views at a time when the papal condemnations of Americanism and Modernism were still potent forces in American Catholic life. In many respects Duffy anticipated by thirty years the pioneering work of John Courtney Murray, who would live to see his own revisionist theology enshrined in the "Declaration on Religious Freedom" of Vatican Council II.

## Governor Smith's Creed As an American Catholic

[From Governor Smith's Statement in The Atlantic Monthly.]

I summarize my creed as an American Catholic:

I believe in the worship of God according to the faith and practice of the Roman Catholic Church. I recognize no power in the institutions of my Church to interfere with the operations of the Constitution of the United States or the enforcement of the law of the land.

I believe in absolute freedom of conscience for all men and in equality of all churches, all sects and all beliefs before the law as a matter of right and not as a matter of favor.

I believe in the absolute separation of Church and State and in the strict enforcement of the provisions of the Constitution that Congress shall make no law respecting an establishment of religion or prohibiting the free exercise thereof.

I believe that no tribunal of any church has any power to make any decree of any force in the law of the land other than to establish the status of its own communicants within its own church.

I believe in the support of the public school as one of the cornerstones of American liberty. I believe in the right of every parent to choose whether his child shall be educated in the public school or in a religious school supported by those of his own faith.

I believe in the principle of non-interference by this country in the internal affairs of other nations and that we should stand steadfastly against any such interference by whomsoever it may be urged.

And I believe in the common brotherhood of man under the common fatherhood of God.

In this spirit I join with fellow-Americans of all creeds in a fervent prayer that never again in this land will any public servant be challenged because of the faith in which he has tried to walk humbly with his God.

Church of the Holy Cross, West 42nd Street in the late Nineteenth Century

Cardinal Hayes appears to be overdressed for the occasion, but, from 1886 until 1929, the Bahamas were under the jurisdiction of the Archdiocese of New York

# The Great Depression

James Francis Cardinal McIntyre, Archbishop of Los Angeles, 1948-1970

The Great Depression had a devastating effect in New York City. By 1932 a third of the city's factories had closed, a quarter of the population was unemployed, and the municipal debt of almost two billion dollars was equal to that of all the 48 states combined. The magnitude of the crisis exhausted the resources of private charity, necessitating unprecedented government assistance. Cardinal Hayes never publicly endorsed the New Deal legislation of President Franklin D. Roosevelt, but neither did he add his voice to the chorus of the President's conservative critics. In fact, his sympathies for such government intervention in the economy were well known. As far back as 1919, when he was still an auxiliary bishop and one of the four members of the administrative board of the National Catholic Welfare Council, Hayes had signed the Bishops' Program for Social Reconstruction, a controversial position paper of the American bishops which advocated many of the reforms enacted into law during the New Deal.

During the Depression Hayes gave his full support to Keegan, an admirer of Roosevelt, who declared in 1933 that "economic forces must be subjected to the law of social justice and industrial life so directed as to promote the welfare of all the people." At the same time Hayes indicated his dislike of Father Charles Coughlin, the demagogic radio priest, through an article that appeared in a prominent clerical periodical, *The Ecclesiastical Review*. The author, Father Edward Dargin, a New York priest, accused Coughlin of violating canon law by his political activities and pointedly denied newspaper reports that the New York Chancery Office had raised no objection to Coughlin's appearance in New York in May 1935 to address a rally of his Union of Social Justice.

It was in the midst of the Great Depression that the liturgical renewal made its first hesitant appearance

in the less than welcoming atmosphere of the New York archdiocese. At Corpus Christi Church in Morningside Heights, the pastor, George Barry Ford, introduced an embryonic form of popular participation. At Sunday Mass, while one priest celebrated the Latin liturgy at the altar, another priest, stationed in the pulpit, provided a translation and running commentary in English. Ford was also a pioneer in ecumenical activity, which aroused deep misgivings in the conservative chancellor, Monsignor J. Francis McIntyre. On one occasion Ford sent a bouquet of flowers to Riverside Church as an anniversary present. When McIntyre heard of it, he asked Ford pointedly: "Is not this a manifestation of brotherhood that borders on *communicatio* [*in sacris*]?"

The liturgical renewal in its early formative years often went hand in hand with a concern for social jus-

tice. The New York diocesan priest who best epitomized that tradition was John Monaghan, a feisty Irish-born cleric who combined a week-end ministry in Corpus Christi Church with a fulltime assignment as teacher and librarian in Cathedral College. There, from 1922 to 1939, he introduced a whole generation of New York's future priests to the social teaching of the Church and instilled in many of them his own love of learning. In 1937 Monaghan was also instrumental in establishing the Association of Catholic Trade Unionists and served for many years as chaplain to the organization. A year earlier, at the suggestion of Father John LaFarge, S.J., the Jesuits had opened the first of their "labor colleges" in New York City, the Xavier Labor School, which would quickly achieve fame under the direction of Philip Carey, S.J., and John Corridan, S.J., the latter of whom was the model for the labor priest in Bud Schulberg's movie *On the Waterfront*. In the 1940s both ACTU and the Xavier Labor School played important roles in eliminating Communist influence in the largely Catholic Transport Workers Union and in combating racketeers in the International Longshoreman's Association. The versatile LaFarge, long active in civil rights work, also helped to establish in 1934 the Catholic Interracial Council of New York.

Perhaps the most famous of all the efforts made by Catholics in New York during the Great Depression first came to light on May Day, 1933, when passers-by in Union Square, then a gathering place for local radicals, noticed a new newspaper on sale for one penny a copy. It was called *The Catholic Worker*. Edited by Dorothy Day, a journalist who had become a Catholic in 1927, the eight-page newspaper was only the most visible part of the Catholic Worker movement, which provided shelters, "houses of hospitality" as Dorothy Day called them, for the homeless and unemployed during the depths of the Depression. The Catholic Worker movement also called attention to unjust working conditions and supported struggling labor unions.

Paradoxically the Catholic Worker movement managed to be at once radical and reactionary. It was radical in the sense that it was independent of hierarchical control, and, as one follower put it, "as far left as one could go within the Church," although Jay Dolan once commented that to define its radicalism was "like trying to bottle a morning fog." The reactionary or romantic dimension was evident in the distaste for modern industrial society and the welfare state, so much so that Catholic labor activist John Cort complained that the movement had a tendency to identify Christianity "with handicrafts and subsistence farming."

Corpus Christi Church

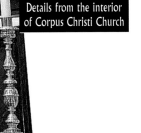
Details from the interior of Corpus Christi Church

The heart of the Catholic Worker movement was Dorothy Day herself, who attracted to her houses of hospitality many young idealistic volunteers like Thomas Merton, Michael Harrington, and Daniel Berrigan, who were eager to experience her own commitment to voluntary poverty and absolute pacifism. Her personal devotion to the poor was a sharp contrast to that of the ever-growing army of government bureaucrats. When a fussy social worker once asked Dorothy Day how long she allowed "clients" to remain in her houses of hospitality, Jim Forest relates that "she answered with a fierce look in her eye" and said, "We let them stay forever. They live with us, they die with us, and we give them a Christian burial. We pray for them after they are dead. Once they are taken in, they become members of the family." Recognized by many as a saint in her own lifetime, Dorothy Day turned away such compliments by saying, "I don't want to be dismissed so easily." "If I have achieved anything in my life," she once remarked, "it is because I have not been embarrassed to talk about God."

Mrs. Coretta Scott King and Dorothy Day at the Cathedral of St. John the Divine in March 1973

# World War II

## AND THE COLD WAR

After the death of Cardinal Hayes on September 4, 1938, seven months elapsed before the appointment of his successor, Francis J. Spellman, the auxiliary bishop of Boston. As Florence Cohalan pointed out, the appointment of Spellman broke a century-old tradition. Ever since the young John Hughes moved into Bishop Dubois' house on Mulberry Street in 1838, every archbishop of New York had spent some time in the entourage of his predecessor. The favored candidate to continue that tradition in 1939 was Stephen J. Donahue, New York's sole auxiliary bishop.

Spellman shattered another tradition as well. Unlike any of his predecessors, he was already a well-known figure when he was selected to be the sixth archbishop of New York. A native of Whitman, Massachusetts, and a graduate of Fordham College and the North American College in Rome, Spellman was ordained a priest of the archdiocese of Boston in Rome on May 14, 1916. For some unexplained reason, young Father Spellman incurred the wrath of William Cardinal O'Connell, the autocratic archbishop of Boston. However, in 1925, he escaped from O'Connell's supervision by using his Roman connections to

Auxiliary Bishop Stephen Donahue and Monsignor Michael Lavelle welcome Archbishop-elect Spellman to New York in May 1939

wrangle a job as the director of the Knights of Columbus playgrounds in Rome, a position which gave him the coveted appointment as an attaché at the Vatican Secretariat of State.

During this second sojourn in Rome, which lasted from 1925 until 1931, Spellman continued his earlier practice of cultivating important people who could advance his own career. He picked his patrons shrewdly, most notably Archbishop Eugenio Pacelli, the nuncio to Weimar Germany. As early as 1927 he wrote to his mother, "All the time I was with him in Berlin, I kept thinking of the great possibilities he has of becoming the next pope."

In 1930 Pacelli became papal secretary of state, and in 1931 Spellman was appointed auxiliary bishop of Boston. Although his relationship with Cardinal O'Connell was strained, Spellman observed the proprieties and bided his time. When Pacelli toured the United States in 1936, Spellman accompanied him across the country and arranged a meeting between Pacelli and President Roosevelt at Hyde Park on November 5, 1936. Pacelli was elected pope on March 2, 1939, and Spellman was appointed the sixth archbishop of New York on April 15, 1939. The first person outside his family to whom he told the news was President Roosevelt.

# Francis Cardinal Spellman

General Douglas Mac Arthur and Archbishop Spellman

Spellman was the most prominent archbishop of New York since John Hughes and probably the best known American prelate since Cardinal Gibbons. From his very first days in New York, he gave evidence of his intention to operate on more than the local level. His friendship with Pius XII gave him an influence in Rome unmatched by any other American bishop or even by the apostolic delegate. At the same time his relationship with Roosevelt assured him of a favored position in the White House, especially after the death on October 2, 1939, of Roosevelt's favorite American Catholic bishop, George Cardinal Mundelein of Chicago. Spellman's stock at the Vatican rose considerably when he played a major role in the negotiations that led to the announcement by Roosevelt on December 24, 1939, three months after the outbreak of the war in Europe, that he would appoint a "personal representative" to the Holy See.

Like Hayes, Spellman also served as the Military Vicar for the Armed Forces, an appointment that he received on December 11, 1939. This position also gave him entrée to a wider world outside New York, especially after the entry of the United States into World War II as a consequence of Pearl Harbor. Every Christmas from 1942 to 1966 Spellman traveled abroad to spend the holidays with American troops overseas. Numerous newspaper photographs of him in military khaki (although he held no rank) visiting the far corners of the world, either smiling from the front seat of a jeep or shaking hands with generals and admirals, made him a familiar and reassuring figure to millions of non-Catholics.

In 1943 he flew to wartime Rome (through neutral Spain), fueling speculation that he was serving as a mediator between the American and Italian governments. He struck a responsive cord with many Americans when he described his chagrin in the Barcelona airport at witnessing a captured American aircraft with Nazi markings take off for Berlin. Spellman's high profile and outspoken patriotism in World War II won him national recognition. In a non-ideological way he managed to achieve the synthesis of loyalty to both church and country that had eluded an earlier generation of "Americanist" bishops like Archbishop John Ireland. In the words of Fr. Gerald P. Fogarty, S.J., Spellman became "the personification of Romanization and Americanzation." On February 18, 1946, at the first postwar consistory, he received the Cardinal's red hat from the hands of Pius XII.

Bishop Spellman accompanied Eugenio Cardinal Pacelli, Papal Secretary of State, on his visit to New York in 1936

Archbishop Spellman celebrating a battlefield Mass during World War II

# Diocesan Administrator

Francis Cardinal Spellman

Spellman's desire to be a national figure meant that he had to rely on subordinates to manage much of the day-to-day administration of the archdiocese. It was a mark of his sense of security that he delegated authority readily without fear of losing control. In his early years he depended heavily on James Francis McIntyre and later on John J. Maguire; both of them in turn were made coadjutor archbishops without the right of succession. A young priest who watched Spellman's arrival in New York in 1939 commented that "only a very superficial observer could miss his intense awareness of his own authority, and his determination that it be recognized and accepted by his subordinates on every level." This same witness, Florence Cohalan, also noted that, despite Spellman's unprecedented distribution of papal honors to the clergy, "he never tried, and presumably never wanted, to put them at ease in his presence."

Under Hayes the archdiocese functioned rather like a feudal kingdom with the pastors enjoying the same autonomy as medieval barons. Spellman transformed them into agents of a centralized monarchy, as Mundelein had already done in Chicago, by means of modern management techniques such as a diocesan bank, insurance office and purchasing agency. Parish reports and financial accounts got closer scrutiny at headquarters than they had received in the past. Like the European nobility in the age of absolutism, the pastors lost real power, but were compensated with a carefully calibrated hierarchy of honorific titles and offices ranging from entry level papal chamberlains to auxiliary bishops, of whom Spellman at one point had an even dozen, their numbers reflecting his power to create and attract them. The most pressing financial problem that Spellman had to face in 1939 was the debt that the archdiocese had accumulated during the Depression. To Spellman's intense annoyance, on the very day of his installation as archbishop, May 23, 1939, he received a patronizing letter from the president of the Emigrant Industrial Savings Bank, informing him that "mortgages in the New York Archdiocese aggregate in the vicinity of $28,000,000." That night, said Spellman's authorized biographer, Father Robert I. Gannon, S.J., "he found himself smoldering and could not sleep until he had planned his first steps in the refinancing of the archdiocese." At his first meeting with the archdiocesan consultors in June, the new archbishop noted dryly that conditions in New York were "entirely different from conditions existing in the diocese from

View of Hudson River from St. Augustine's Church, Ossining

Cardinal Hayes High School, the first of New York's diocesan high schools

which I come." Within a month, with the help of McIntyre, he had refinanced the debt by negotiating better terms from bankers in both New York and Boston, and he calculated that he had already saved the archdiocese $500,000 per year in interest payments.

World War II forced Spellman to defer most of his building projects. During his first eight years in New York, for example, he opened only three new parishes, St. Gabriel's in Riverdale (1939), St. Helena's in the East Bronx (1940) adjacent to the mammoth new Parkchester housing complex, and Our Lady of Victory (1944), a "business" parish in the heart of the downtown

financial district. It was an indication of Spellman's business acumen that he personally selected the site for the new parish in Riverdale and purchased it for the bargain price of $190,000 before issuing the public announcement, which would have driven up real estate values.

Even before Pearl Harbor, Spellman began one of his most innovative contributions when he decided to organize a diocesan high school system. On an unpromising piece of real estate overlooking a railroad yard in the South Bronx, Spellman built an architecturally stunning school, which he named in honor of his predecessor.

Cardinal Hayes High School opened its doors in 1941 with a faculty of 42 diocesan priests, 47 brothers and four laymen. During its first 50 years, it graduated some 23,000 students, among them 500 priests and brothers, 700 firefighters and 1,000 policemen. Spellman was interested in more than brick and mortar. He encouraged priest-teachers to earn graduate degrees and subsidized their studies generously from diocesan funds. In 1942 Spellman also moved Cathedral College to more spacious quarters on West End Avenue and later sold the old college building on Madison Avenue for a whopping $2,800,000.

# Postwar America

Immediately after the war, the archdiocese embarked on a large-scale expansion of its educational facilities. By 1952, 134 elementary and high schools had either been built, renovated or were in the planning stages. The building campaign accelerated in the later 1950s. Between 1953 and 1959, the archdiocese constructed or expanded 15 churches, 94 schools, 22 rectories, 60 convents and 30 other institutions, at a total cost of $139,700,000. The G.I. Bill of Rights put a college education within reach of many working-class Catholic families. As a result Fordham University and Manhattan College both experienced big increases in enrollment, as did Iona College in New Rochelle, which had been founded by the Irish Christian Brothers in 1940.

The postwar decades also witnessed a proliferation of new Catholic colleges throughout the country.

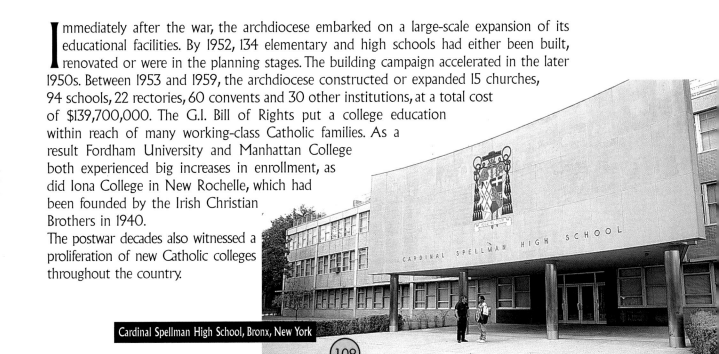
Cardinal Spellman High School, Bronx, New York

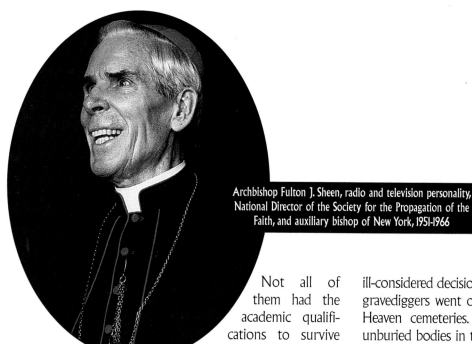

Archbishop Fulton J. Sheen, radio and television personality, National Director of the Society for the Propagation of the Faith, and auxiliary bishop of New York, 1951-1966

Not all of them had the academic qualifications to survive the rigors of the succeeding decades, but three that did in the New York archdiocese date from the 1950s, Dominican College of Blauvelt, St. Thomas Aquinas College in Sparkill, and Mount St. Mary's College in Newburgh. At St. Joseph's Seminary, Dunwoodie, Spellman spent several million dollars on renovations that included a new library and gymnasium, earning the right to be called the second founder of Dunwoodie.

Health care and social services were also expanded. The showpiece of the Catholic hospital system was St. Vincent's Hospital in Greenwich Village, the city's oldest Catholic hospital. Beginning with the addition of the Spellman wing in 1941, the hospital, under the direction of the Sisters of Charity, kept expanding its facilities until it developed into a major medical center with almost 900 beds.

Although Spellman's influence at the White House waned after Harry Truman replaced Roosevelt as president in 1945, he still commanded national attention as an outspoken foe of Communism at home and abroad. To call attention to the Communist persecution of the Church in Eastern Europe, a new diocesan high school in White Plains was named after Archbishop Aloysius Stepinac, the victim of a show trial staged by the Yugoslav government. Spellman's suspicions of Communism led him to make one of the most

ill-considered decisions of his career in 1949 when the gravediggers went on strike in Calvary and Gate of Heaven cemeteries. Before long, there were 1,000 unburied bodies in the two cemeteries. Persuaded by his advisers that a Communist-controlled labor union was responsible for the crisis, the Cardinal broke the strike by bringing in seminarians from Dunwoodie to work as substitute gravediggers. Many Catholics applauded his action, but many others were appalled, among them John Cort, one of the founders of ACTU, who complained that "rightly or wrongly [it] puts the Church in the role of strikebreaker and union-buster." Spellman, however, was not the least bit apologetic. "I admit to the accusation of strikebreaker," he said, "and I am proud of it."

That same year the Cardinal became involved in an ugly public dispute with Mrs. Eleanor Roosevelt over the issue of federal aid to parochial schools. When she announced her opposition to such aid in her syndicated newspaper column, the Cardinal took issue with her in an open letter and characterized her position as "discrimination unworthy of an American mother." Mrs. Roosevelt had the better of the exchange when she replied, "The final judgment, my dear Cardinal Spellman, of the unworthiness of all human beings is in the hands of God." A few weeks later Spellman visited Mrs. Roosevelt at her Hyde Park residence, and the next day they both issued "clarifying" statements.

Anti-Communist fervor also led the Cardinal to give at least tacit endorsement to Senator Joseph McCarthy. On April 4, 1954, with the senator in attendance, he presided at the annual Mass in St. Patrick's Cathedral for the Holy Name Society of the New York City Police Department. After the Mass he was present at the Communion breakfast at which McCarthy was the principal speaker, a gesture which was widely interpreted as a sign of support for the controversial Senator.

Cardinal Spellman and Pope Pius XII

Dunwoodie seminarians digging graves in Calvary cemetery during the 1949 strike

Gerald Fogarty has pointed out, the path to such power was barred by three midwestern prelates, Samuel Stritch of Chicago, Edward Mooney of Detroit and John McNicholas of Cincinnati. Together they dominated the leadership of the National Catholic Welfare Conference, the national agency of the American bishops, and they combined to form what they called the Hindenburg Line, a *cordon sanitaire* to keep Spellman's influence confined to the East Coast. With the exception of McIntyre's appointment to Los Angeles, they succeeded admirably.

Although Spellman's influence in Washington declined after 1945, it remained as powerful as ever in Rome, as was evident from the number of important episcopal appointments that he was able to engineer. Patrick O'Boyle, head of Catholic Charities in New York, became the first archbishop of Washington in 1947; James Francis McIntyre became the archbishop of Los Angeles a year later; John O'Hara, CSC, auxiliary bishop in the Military Ordinariate, became bishop of Buffalo in 1945 and archbishop of Philadelphia in 1951. All three were later made cardinals.

Perhaps the high water mark of Spellman's role as king-maker occurred in 1957 when the new diocese of Rockville Centre was created on Long Island after the death of Archbishop Thomas Molloy of Brooklyn. Both dioceses were filled by New Yorkers, Bryan McEntegart and Walter Kellenberg. Even during the heyday of his ascendancy in Rome under Pius XII, however, the Cardinal never quite made good his claim to inherit the mantle of James Cardinal Gibbons and become the unofficial primate of the American Catholic Church. As Father

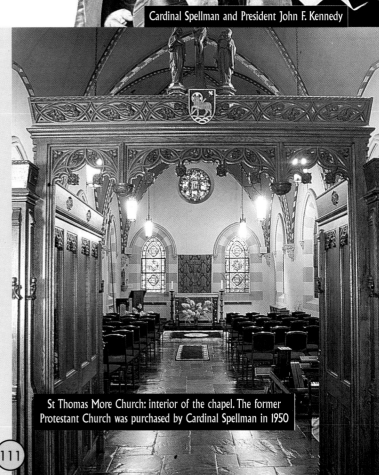

Cardinal Spellman and President John F. Kennedy

# The Puerto Rican Migration

The greatest pastoral challenge facing the archdiocese in the postwar years was the influx of several hundred thousand Puerto Rican immigrants, who transformed many of the old Irish and German parishes in Manhattan and the Bronx into solidly Hispanic neighborhoods. It was a test that Spellman passed with flying colors. First of all, he sought and accepted good advice, especially from his chancellor, John J. Maguire, who was quick to recognize the dimensions of the problem, and from two young priest-sociologists, George A. Kelly, and Joseph P. Fitzpatrick, S.J., of Fordham University. In a scientific study begun in 1952, Kelly estimated that the Puerto Rican population of the archdiocese would reach 800,000 by 1960 and he called particular attention to the need for Spanish-speaking priests.

St Thomas More Church: interior of the chapel. The former Protestant Church was purchased by Cardinal Spellman in 1950

Good Shepherd window, St Thomas More Church

Spellman made two fundamental policy decisions in the early 1950s. First, he abandoned the hallowed tradition of national parishes for each ethnic group in favor of all-inclusive integrated parishes for the Puerto Ricans. Secondly, he decided that his own diocesan priests rather than the religious orders should assume the main responsibility for the pastoral care of the Puerto Ricans. According to sociologist Ana Maria Diaz-Stevens, herself a participant in the great Puerto Rican migration to the mainland, "Spellman's greatest contribution to the New York archdiocese in its policy toward the Puerto Ricans was to recognize the missionary character of the situation."

In the course of 1953 the Cardinal gave clear indications of his commitment to the apostolate by establishing a new Office of Spanish Catholic Action and by sending the first New York diocesan priests to learn Spanish. In future years as many as half of the newly ordained priests were sent to Puerto Rico to study the language and culture at the Catholic University of Puerto Rico. Beginning in 1953 the archdiocese sponsored an annual San Juan Fiesta on June 24 to commemorate the island's patron saint. In 1957 Spellman informed the apostolic delegate that the population of Manhattan was now one-third Puerto Rican. "I do not know whether this information is important to the Holy See," he added, "but it is certainly significant to us." By the following year the archdiocese had over 200 Spanish-speaking priests, and approximately one-quarter of the parishes were providing religious services in Spanish. Direction of the apostolate remained firmly in diocesan hands. The first four coordinators of the office of Spanish Catholic Action—Joseph Connolly, James Wilson, Robert Fox, and Robert Stern—were New York priests and fluent Spanish speakers. And hovering over the whole operation as vice rector of the Catholic University of Puerto Rico was the charismatic figure of Ivan Illich, a Yugoslav-born priest whom Spellman accepted into the archdiocese in 1952. Reviewing the results of a sociological survey published by the archdiocese in 1982, Joseph Fitzpatrick commented on the overwhelmingly favorable attitude to the Catholic Church manifested by most Hispanics in New York, and he attributed it largely to the work of the clergy and religious over the previous thirty years.

The San Juan Fiesta in the late 1960s, left to right:
Fr. Joseph Fitzpatrick, S.J., Auxiliary Bishop Terence Cooke,
Fr. Gerald Ryan, Cardinal Spellman and Msgr. Thomas O'Brien

Aerial view of the San Juan Fiesta,
Randall's Island, in June 1961

# Winds of Change

Spellman's last years as archbishop coincided with dramatic and far-reaching changes in both the Catholic Church and American society. The catalyst for many of the changes in the Church was Vatican Council II, which met in Rome for several months each autumn between 1962 and 1965. Over 2,000 bishops were present at the sessions of the council as well as an unprecedented number of official non-Catholic observers. As the senior American cardinal and one of the council presidents, Spellman played a significant role in Vatican Council II, making more interventions than any other American prelate. Generally he aligned himself with the conservatives, especially in his opposition to liturgical changes. Even in this area, however, he showed a streak of independence by favoring permission for priests to use the vernacular in the recitation of the breviary. The most significant American contribution to the Council was almost certainly the "Declaration on Religious Freedom."

Cardinal Spellman vested for
Mass in St. Patrick Cathedral

Spellman supported it vigorously and, even more importantly, he played a crucial role in bringing to Rome for the second session of the Council one of the principal architects of that document, Father John Courtney Murray, S.J. "My eminent friend of New York," Murray called Spellman after the Cardinal rescued him from the limbo to which his own religious superiors had consigned him.

Spellman also defied facile ideological classification by showing a surprising openness to modern biblical scholarship. Personalities may have been as big a factor as the issues in shaping Spellman's views, but, nonetheless, he came to the defense of Father Patrick Skehan, a New York priest who was professor of Semitic Languages at the Catholic University of America, when he tangled with Father Joseph Fenton, an archconservative and politically well-connected theologian at the university. Spellman reassured both Archbishop Patrick O'Boyle of Washington and the Apostolic Delegate, Archbishop Egidio Vagnozzi, that he had "great esteem" for Skehan and "complete confidence" in him. Spellman was equally supportive of Father Myles Bourke, professor of Scripture at St. Joseph's Seminary, Dunwoodie. Both Bourke and Richard Dillon, then a seminarian at Dunwoodie and editor of the newly-founded *Dunwoodie Review*, came under fire from Alfredo Cardinal Ottaviani, the powerful prefect of the Holy Office. Spellman rebuffed Ottaviani's suggestion that he should dismiss Bourke from the Dunwoodie faculty. Instead, he told Bourke in writing: "I have complete confidence in you and consider you a great asset to St. Joseph's Seminary." Spellman and Cardinal McIntyre of Los Angeles were often lumped together as ideological fellow travelers, but Spellman's receptivity to modern biblical scholarship was a source of puzzlement to McIntyre. He revealed his misgivings to Spellman when they were Rome together for the Council. "That you seem to be impressed with this thinking," McIntyre told Spellman, "is—I must be frank—is somewhat shocking to me."

Sisters in full habits
before Vatican Council II

During the turbulent 1960s, the decade when everything seemed to go wrong, Spellman sometimes took positions that surprised his liberal critics, although he got little credit from them for doing so. In October 1960 the Catholic bishops of Puerto Rico dropped a bombshell into the presidential election of that year when they warned the Catholics of the island not to vote for the Popular Democratic Party of Governor Luis Muñoz-Marin. Spellman helped to defuse the situation and spare John F. Kennedy considerable embarrassment by stating publicly that the Catholics of Puerto Rico would not be committing a sin, if they voted contrary to the bishops' wishes. Five years later, in response to a query from the Apostolic Delegate, Spellman also defended the right of priests and religious to take part in civil rights demonstrations, asserting that such participation in his archdiocese had "evoked widespread approval as indicating sympathetic involvement of congregations and communities in favor of human and civil rights." Perhaps the most gratifying day in Spellman's twenty-eight years as archbishop of New York occurred on October 4, 1965, when Pope Paul VI became the first pope to visit the New World. The formal occasion was the twentieth anniversary of the United Nations. Papal visits anywhere outside of Rome were still rare and unusual

events, and Pope Paul had decided to limit his trip to a one-day whirlwind visit. From the moment the pontiff landed at Idlewild airport (as it was still called) until his departure that evening, Spellman never left his side. A fast-moving motorcade whisked the pope on a twenty-five mile tour through Queens and upper Manhattan to St. Patrick's Cathedral where the formal liturgical reception took place in the presence of 5,000 guests, with another 50,000 people gathered in the streets outside the cathedral. That afternoon Pope Paul paid a courtesy call on President Lyndon Johnson at the Waldorf-Astoria, and then addressed the General Assembly of the United Nations where he made an impassioned plea for peace ("no more war, never again war"), and lauded the United Nations as "the last hope of peace." Afterwards the pontiff attended an ecumenical service at the Church of the Holy Family on East Forty-Seventh Street. That evening the pope celebrated an outdoor Mass in Yankee Stadium before 92,000 wor-

Crucifixion scene, St. Joseph's Church, Bronxville

shippers and stopped to visit the Vatican Pavilion at the World's Fair before boarding his plane for Rome. As the euphoria of the pope's visit faded, however, the winds of change began to blow more briskly through both the Church and the country. Spellman found it increasingly difficult to adjust to the new landscape. "The [liturgical] changes are too many and too soon," he told his old Roman friend, Count Enrico Galeazzi, a few months before the pope's visit. "I am having a difficult time," he admitted to Galeazzi, and he added: "I do not think that things in Rome could be any more 'dizzy'

St. Joseph's Church, Bronxville

Interior of St. Joseph's Church, Bronxville

than they are here in the United States." In Rome the pope was also having a difficult time as he tried to steer the bark of Peter between extremists on the right and on the left. He chided those who resisted the liturgical changes, telling them, "Before it was enough to attend; today it is necessary to participate." At the same time the pope lashed out at what he called the spirit of "radical reformism" that threatened the doctrinal integrity of the Church.

Whatever his personal reservations, Spellman began the implementation of the conciliar changes in New York. In keeping with the emphasis on decentralization, he established six vicariates with an auxiliary bishop in charge of each. He also agreed to the creation of a Senate of Priests with forty-nine elected members, and approved the formation of two experimental parishes where authority was vested in a team of priests rather than in an individual pastor. At age seventy-seven, Spellman was two years past the newly instituted retirement age for bishops. In the fall of 1966, he duly offered his resignation to Paul VI, but the pope rejected it and asked him to remain as archbishop.

Perhaps even more than the post-conciliar changes, the Vietnam War was a traumatic event for Spellman. In the summer of 1965 a somber President Johnson told the American people: "This is really war." Like many Americans of his generation, Spellman equated this war with America's involvement in World War II and could not comprehend the reasons for the domestic opposition to it. He remained a staunch supporter of the war to the end of his life, continuing his holiday visits to American troops overseas and declaring in 1966 that "total victory means peace." Shortly before his death, antiwar protestors (including some nuns) disrupted Sunday Mass in St. Patrick's Cathedral. It was an incomprehensible development for many American Catholics who had grown to maturity in an earlier era when faith and patriotism were unquestioning allies.

When Spellman died on December 2, 1967, events beyond his control had left him more and more alienated from the Church and country that he loved deeply.

Cardinal Spellman and Pope Paul VI

# New York Catholicism

## AFTER VATICAN II

**T**erence James Cooke was appointed the seventh archbishop of New York on March 2, 1968, replacing Cardinal Spellman after the shortest vacancy in the history of the see. His appointment caused general surprise, if not astonishment, especially among the clientage of John J. Maguire, the coadjutor archbishop without the right of succession. Only 47 years old and an auxiliary bishop for less than three years, Cooke hardly seemed to have been a serious contender for the post, especially since he lacked

Terence Cardinal Cooke

the Roman political connections deemed essential for such an appointment. Pundits attributed his selection to Spellman's influence *d'outre tombe*. As expected, the new archbishop quickly received two additional honors. He was appointed Military Vicar for the Armed Forces on the day of his installation, April 4, 1968, and he was made a Cardinal one year later, on April 28, 1969.

Terence Cooke was a native New Yorker, the son of Irish immigrant parents, who named him after the Irish nationalist hero Terence McSwiney, the Lord Mayor of Cork, who died on a hunger strike in a British prison in 1920. Born in Manhattan on March 1, 1921, and raised in the Bronx, young Terence followed the traditional New York path to the diocesan priesthood, education at Cathedral College and St. Joseph's Seminary, Dunwoodie, followed by ordination at St. Patrick's Cathedral by Cardinal Spellman on December 1, 1945. After brief stints in pastoral work, Father Cooke was sent to the Catholic University of America where he earned a M.S.W. degree. Upon his return to New York, he spent the following four years in the Catholic Youth Organization. In 1954 he was made procurator of St. Joseph's Seminary, Dunwoodie, where his talents came to the attention of Cardinal Spellman. Thereafter Cooke's star ascended rapidly in the ecclesiastical firmament as he moved up the ranks from Spellman's secretary to vice-chancellor, chancellor, vicar

President Ronald Reagan and Cardinal Cooke

116

general, and in 1965 auxiliary bishop. Cooke was a warm and friendly man with a prodigious memory and an extraordinary capacity for hard work. As his close friend, Bishop Patrick V. Ahern, put it, "He was just, in his own words, 'a boy from the Bronx,' with an accent to prove it." Terence Cooke was not in any sense a visionary. He dreamed no great dreams and expressed no passionately held opinions about what new kind of Catholic Church might emerge from Vatican Council II. If anything, he seems

Nativity scene, St Ann's Church, Yonkers

to have hoped that the post-Vatican II Church would look very much like the pre-Vatican II Church. "Let us improve the institutions that have served us so well," he said at his installation. "Let us avoid that iconoclasm which would tear down the past before moving ahead in the present to build a future."

As the leader of what the *New York Times* persisted in calling "the world's wealthiest archdiocese," Cooke was automatically an important figure, but he never exerted the same influence as Spellman on either the national or international scene. No one recognized the difference more clearly than he did himself. He told an interviewer in 1973, "I don't think my key role is to be a leader in national or international affairs." His fellow bishops elected him chairman of the U.S. Bishops' Pro-Life Activities Committee. In that capacity, Cooke worked vigorously to combat the rising tide of abortions in the United States, especially after the U.S. Supreme Court swept away most of the legal barriers to abortion in the *Roe v. Wade* decision of 1973. Cooke also served as spokesman for the U.S. bishops on the question of tax credits for the parents of parochial school children, and he chaired a committee to devise a system of uniform accounting for U.S. dioceses.

However, Cooke made his main contribution to the American Church in his own native city, bringing to the task of archbishop of New York two qualities vitally needed at that time, managerial skills and pastoral sensitivity. A long apprenticeship under Spellman had left Cooke thoroughly familiar with the operations of the archdiocese when he assumed the reins in 1968. "When I take on a job," he said, "I try to do my homework." "He loves annual reports," said one of his advisors. "He can sit with a seventy-page memo on how to rescue the hospitals and master it." That facet of his personality surfaced at the 200 board meetings that he regularly attended each year, when

Cooke often astonished the bankers and businessmen in attendance with his detailed knowledge of the financial condition of each institution. He excelled not only at managing money, but also at raising it. One pastor commented that "he's the kind of guy who can pat you on the back until the change falls out of your pockets."

Much as Cooke excelled as the CEO of the archdiocese, he regarded himself primarily as a pastor. "I don't want to be a politician," he said on one occasion. "I have enough problems already." "My job, first and foremost," he explained, "is to be a shepherd and servant of God's people. I have no other purpose or desire in life." While critics complained of his lack of vision ("He has no message," observed one disgruntled Chancery official), Cooke's pastoral sensitivity led him to prefer consensus to confrontation at a time of growing polarization in the Church among both clergy and laity. "He managed to provide a context within which a lot of viewpoints could be at home," said Monsignor Philip Murnion, director of the National Pastoral Life Office. "People could pursue a variety of interests." "He allows many flowers to grow," observed Fr. James Connolly in 1975, "even though he may not like them all."

Cardinal Cooke in October 1982 with the first-grade children in St. Athanasius school, the parish where he served briefly as a young curate shortly after ordination

# Church and Country after Vatican Council II

Cooke's baptism of fire began on the day of his installation as archbishop of New York, April 4, 1968, which was the same day that Dr. Martin Luther King, Jr., was assassinated in Memphis. By nightfall riots had erupted in many cities across the country, including New York City. That evening the new archbishop left a reception in his honor to travel to Harlem where he pleaded for calm and peace. Two months after Cooke's installation, St. Patrick's Cathedral was again jammed with worshippers, including the President of the United States, this time for the funeral Mass of Senator Robert F. Kennedy, the victim of another assassin.

The unfinished agenda of the civil rights movement, the unpopularity of the Vietnam War, and then the Watergate scandal all combined to produce one of the most tumultuous periods in modern American history. Public discontent reached such proportions that the President of the United States could not appear in public without provoking widespread protest demonstrations, especially from young Americans. In this atmosphere, all forms of authority, religious as well as political, were called into question, often to be subjected to searing scrutiny, sometimes to be rejected with cynical derision.

At the same time that the nation was experiencing this crisis of confidence, the Catholic Church was contending with equally serious problems. The effort to implement the conciliar reforms often produced jarring dislocations in a Church that had no living tradition of candid criticism or devolution of authority, illustrating once again Tocqueville's famous dictum that the most difficult period for a government is when it begins to make reforms. Cooke treaded his way gingerly through this minefield, taking his cue from Pope Paul VI, and like the pope, trying to find a middle path between the reformers and the reactionaries.

Even those two nebulous political labels became more fluid and harder to define as some of the more progressive figures at the time of the Council now drew back in consternation at unexpected developments such as the decline in Mass attendance, the falling off in vocations, the sharp increase in resignations from the priesthood and religious life, the growing demand for

optional clerical celibacy, and the first murmurs of women's ordination movement. The hostile reception given to *Humanae Vitae*, Pope Paul's encyclical of 1968 reaffrming the prohibition against contraception, only increased fears that the Church's authority was in the process of disintegration. "Unless we are blind," said Louis Bouyer, the French Catholic scholar, in a book published that year, "we must state bluntly that what we see looks less like the hoped-for regeneration of Catholicism than its accelerated decomposition."

Jean Cardinal Daniélou gave voice to these same apprehensions at the Synod of Bishops in the fall of 1969, when he declared: "The state of the Church today is no longer that existing during Vatican II…. We are witnesses today… of a very grave crisis." He called for "firm and unique authority." Léon-Joseph Cardinal Suenens, however, warned against a return to a nineteenth-century concept of papal authority that would leave no room for the collegial leadership of pope and bishops envisioned by the Council.

St. Anthony's Shrine Church, Nanuet

It is significant that the expression of such views only four years after the end of the Council had already become so suspect that Suenens had to assure a group of journalists that "there are no heretics here."

John Cardinal Wright, the former bishop of Pittsburgh and now a curial official, fully shared Daniélou's fears. On his way to the synod, he left a note for Cooke at 452 Madison Avenue. "Your Eminence," the message read, "I stopped today to say 'Hi' on the way from the worries at home to the worries in Rome. They are about the same, so I might as well go back to the office." Earlier that year Wright had been one of the architects of a pastoral letter of the U.S. bishops that gave a grim assessment of the state of the American Church. The optimism that had been pervasive among the American bishops during the Council had now given way to alarm that they were losing their ability to direct the shape and pace of reform. "Many of us think we see an unfortunate eclipse of the clear and separate status of ordained priesthood," the bishops warned. Stunned by the unprecedented number of resignations from the active ministry, they lashed out at such priests as "derelict" and a source of scandal to the laity. However, the bishops reserved their heaviest thunder for what they called "a new Pelagianism [that] seeks salvation in the

Window of Our Lady, Immaculate Heart of Mary Church, Scarsdale

correction of structures rather than in conversion to God."

One of the signers of the pastoral letter was Archbishop Cooke, who was faced with a demand for new structures in his own diocese. Even before his appointment had been announced, 563 priests had signed a petition asking the pope for some role in the selection of their new archbishop. They had couched their request in extremely deferential language. "With sentiments of profound respect and filial obedience," they told Pope Paul, "we make bold to address to Your Holiness these few words concerning our bishop and our diocese." However respectful the rhetoric, the fact that priests even dared to make such a request was an indication that the forelock touching days were over. "We wanted to express our opinion and be consulted," said Fr. Neil Connolly matter of factly.

Once it became clear that Cooke was to be the new archbishop, he was presented with a Memorandum of Priorities by the Priests' Interim Advisory Committee, which was the name adopted by the Senate of Priests when their mandate lapsed during the interregnum between Spellman and Cooke. Among the requests of the Advisory Committee was that Cooke should dis-

Interior of Immaculate Heart of Mary Church, Scarsdale

Chapel of Corpus Christi Monnastery, home of a community of cloistered contemplative Dominican Sisters in the South Bronx

Interior scenes, St. Augustine's Church, Larchmont

close the financial condition of the archdiocese, consult the priests on the appointment of diocesan officials, appoint an Archdiocesan Pastoral Council, and establish a diocesan department of urban affairs. Cooke eyed the Advisory Committee with the same wariness that Louis XVI had once displayed before the Estates General, especially after a spokesman for the priests declared that the archdiocese of New York showed "some of the classic signs of revolution". A master of the soft answer that turns away wrath but concedes nothing, Cooke described the report as "just suggestions" from a "really terrific group of priests."

Cooke displayed the same finesse at a potentially embarrassing situation in 1971 during the annual ordination of Jesuit seminarians to the

priesthood. Two of the newly ordained Jesuits refused to exchange the traditional sign of peace with Cooke as a protest over his role as Military Vicar. Unfazed, Cooke explained that he worked for peace every day even in his capacity as Military Vicar and invited the two protestors to reconsider their snub. One of them did and came forward to shake Cooke's hand. The other still refused, and to him Cooke said quietly, "Peace to you, especially, my friend."

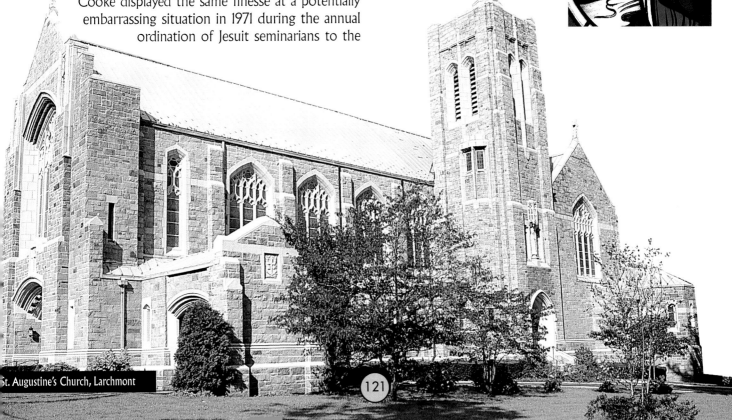

St. Augustine's Church, Larchmont

# The South Bronx

One area of the archdiocese that received massive media attention in the 1970s was the South Bronx, which became a symbol of the problems of America's inner cities. The *New York Times* declared that a visit to the area was "as crucial to the understanding of American urban life as a visit to Auschwitz is to understanding Nazism." It included the poorest Congressional district in the nation, a police station that was known as Fort Apache, and Charlotte Street, a burnt-out stretch of rubble and decay that became a mandatory photo stop for Presidential candidates. A visitor to Charlotte Street in 1968, Adele Chatfield Taylor, called it "a place beyond description [where] wild dogs roamed the streets, tearing in and out of buildings, and through the trash that covered the sidewalks and the buildings. Persons scarcely recognizable as human were prey and predator to one another. Fires burned everywhere."

As Jill Jonnes, the historian of the Bronx , has pointed out, the designation "South Bronx" became "a traveling curse" in the 1970s, as crime, arson and the abandonment of buildings spread from the original South Bronx, a one square mile section of Mott Haven, to Melrose, Morrisania, Hunt's Point, West Farms, Tremont, Highbridge and Morris Heights, until the plague engulfed twenty square miles of the borough south of Fordham Road. In 1960, there were 11,185 fires in the Bronx; in 1974, 33,465 fires. During the worst period of the Bronx's trial by fire, Jonnes also notes: "The Catholic Church quietly emerged as the institution most committed to preserving and resurrecting the benighted South Bronx. Not one church or Catholic school [was] closed." Edward J. Logue, the head of New York City's South Bronx Development Organization and a professional builder, thought that the Catholic clergy played an indispensable role in saving the South Bronx. He was especially warm in his praise of Fr. Louis Gigante's efforts to rebuild the devastated Hunt's Point area in St. Athanasius parish. Logue gave Gigante's South East Bronx Community Organization credit for completing "the most successful critical mass of neighborhood rebuilding in the whole city." Fr. Neil Connolly, the vicar of the South Bronx, led a coalition that pressured the district attorney and the borough president to institute a special Bronx Task Force in 1975 to combat arson. South Bronx Churches, a later coalition of Protestant and Catholic clergy, taught poor people how to use their political muscle to obtain better housing and stem the decline of their neighborhoods.

In the mid-1970s other priests helped to organize the Northwest Bronx Community and Clergy Coalition, using their influence to prevent panic flight and the spread of arson and abandonment to the rest of the Bronx. They enlisted the services of Bishop Patrick V. Ahern, the vicar of the Northwest Bronx, who visited the parishes of the area, speaking at the Sunday Masses and telling the people: "If the Bronx dies, then the hopes of a million and a half people for justice and a decent

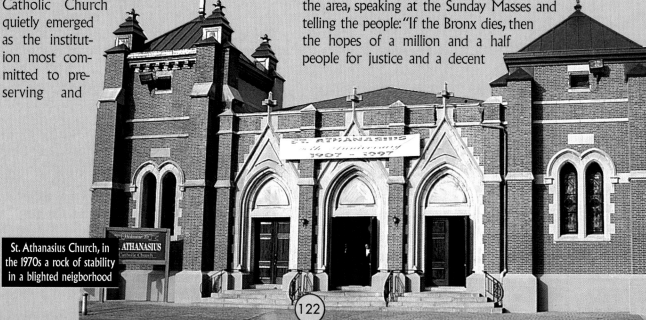

Abandonned buildings: a familiar scene in the South Bronx in the 1970s

St. Athanasius Church, in the 1970s a rock of stability in a blighted neigborhood

life will die with it. We're trying to stop that from happening."

By the 1980s the worst of the arson was over, if only because there was little left to burn. Fort Apache, standing amid the rubble, was renamed the Little House on the Prairie. Slowly but surely the Bronx began to rebuild and recover. Commenting on the situation in 1985, Senator Daniel Patrick Moynihan said: "After much travail, and much failure, and much avoidance of the obvious, the people of the South Bronx and the Catholic Church got together and have set to work. And the Lord's work it is."

A major reason for the Church's credibility in the South Bronx was the fact that the priests and religious who staffed the churches, schools and social agencies not only worked in the area but lived

there. Many of them were natives of the Bronx, not naïve dilettantes, but street-smart people, who had grown up in solidly middle-class neighborhoods and remained to minister to a predominantly poor Hispanic and African American population. An outstanding but not untypical example is Msgr. Gerald Ryan, who, in 1999, had spent a total of 54 years in two South Bronx parishes. "You have to allow circumstances to change you," he said modestly. "I really feel that the South Bronx has more for me than I have done for the South Bronx."

# Calmer Waters

In the course of Cooke's first few years as archbishop, many of the recommendations of the Priests' Advisory Council were adopted in one form or another, but with few of the results either anticipated or feared. Other changes followed as well. In 1970 Cooke established the Commission for Inter-Parish Financing, which levied a tax of six or seven percent on all parishes and used the proceeds to assist financially ailing ones. In the first year of its operation, it distributed $2,900,000 to 53 needy parishes; by 1979, the total funds disbursed reached $26 million. Cooke also created the Inner-City Scholarship Fund, which was soon providing subsidies of over one million dollars per year for the tuition of minority students (two-thirds of them non-Catholic) in parochial schools. Thanks to such innovative financial strategies, only 20 of the 294 parochial elementary schools were closed during Cooke's years as archbishop despite a massive decline in enrollment (from 157,435 in 1968 to 88,753 in 1983) and the departure from the schools of three-quarters of the 4,000 teaching sisters. Not all of the changes were financial.

The Resurrection of the South Bronx: new houses on Fox Street in St. Athanasius parish

Sister Mary Alfred, R.S.M., prepares youngs scouts for the procession at the 100ᵗʰ anniversary celebration of Sacred Heart Church, Highbridge, in 1975

Priests complained that they had to wait as long as thirty years to become pastors. In response to this complaint, beginning in 1971, pastors were appointed for only six-year terms with the possibility of renewal for another six-year term. By that date parish councils were functioning in most parishes, and an Archdiocesan Pastoral Council had also been established. In 1972 the archdiocese issued its long-awaited financial report, listing its net worth at $643 million, a deceptively inflated figure because nine-tenths of the archdiocesan assets consisted of real estate of questionable market value. By 1975 much of the post-conciliar turmoil had subsided, and Cooke could breathe a sigh of relief. Commenting on the condition of his archdiocese in that year, he said: "Though it runs a temperature once in a while, it is basically very healthy." The year 1978 was the year of the three popes.

Paul VI died at the age of eighty on August 6; John Paul I, elected on August 26, died thirty-four days later on September 28; John Paul II, the first non-Italian pope in 455 years, was elected on October 16. After triumphal trips to his native Poland and to Mexico, John Paul II made a week-long visit to the United States in 1979. He spent two days in New York, addressing the United Nations where he repeated Pope Paul's plea for world peace. At a prayer service for priests and nuns at St. Patrick's Cathedral, he said: "I consider it a special grace to come back to New York," a city that he had visited as the Archbishop of Krakow in 1976. A rally for school children in Madison Square Garden drew a capacity crowd of 19,000. The pope's intinerary included a visit to Harlem where Monsignor Emerson Moore, the pastor of

St. Charles Borromeo Church, welcomed him by saying: "We see in your visit here your support and encouragement for our continuing struggle for justice and human rights, not just in our own community, but in all the Harlems in America." The pontiff also made a brief stop in the South Bronx where he spoke in Spanish as well as English. Fr. Neil Connolly, told him: "Your presence here tonight means that we count." Said one ecstatic woman, "If the politicians don't care about us, at least God loves us." One of the highlights of the pope's visit to New York was a Mass at Yankee Stadium before 80,000 people. The crowd was smaller than the one that had turned out for Pope Paul fourteen years earlier, but so attentive that one could hear the sound of the elevated train rattling by on the tracks beyond center field. The changes in the liturgy since the previous papal visit were especially noticeable. The scriptural readings were in Spanish and English, the intercessory petitions were offered in nine languages, and it would now have been

Pope John Paul II greets the crowds upon his arrival at Yankee Stadium in 1979

unthinkable not to give everyone an opportunity to receive Holy Communion.

A major demographic change took place in New York City during the Cooke years. Between 1970 and 1980 the city lost 1,750,000 residents, mostly middle class people of older European stock, who fled in droves from areas like the South Bronx. They were replaced by Hispanics, African Americans and immigrants from Asia. By 1980 there were two million Hispanics and two million African Americans in New York City, in addition to growing numbers of immigrants from Japan, China, Korea, Pakistan, India and the Philippines. "The city has always been a city of newcomers," said Fr. Joseph Fitzpatrick, an expert on immigration, "but never did it have such a variety in such numbers crowding into it in such a short time." In the archdiocese, between 1968 and 1983, the overall Catholic population fell by about 30,000 to 1,839,000.

The decline would have been much greater except for the large-scale influx of Hispanics and other Catholic immigrants. However, many of the newcomers were poor and not regular church-goers. In St. Jerome's parish in the South Bronx, attendance at Sunday Mass fell from 6,100 in 1950 to 795 in 1975. "Bulldozers, arson, drugs and white flight had changed the area almost beyond recognition," said Father James Hynes, the historian of the parish. In the archdiocese as a whole, the number of baptisms fell from 53,102 in 1968 to 33,050 in 1983, and the number of marriages from 16,065 to 10,235.

On March 1, 1983, Terence Cooke celebrated his sixty-second birthday. His outward demeanor was as cheerful and effervescent as ever. "He's the most ebullient man you'd meet," said Monsignor Florence Cohalan. "He doesn't like to admit the existence of problems." Less than six months later, on August

27, the archdiocese shocked usually unflappable New Yorkers by announcing that the Cardinal was terminally ill with cancer, a disease that he had been secretly battling for a number of years. He died at his residence forty-one days later, on October 6, 1983.

For someone who was essentially a local rather than a national figure, the outpouring of mourners was exceptionally large. Huge crowds filed past his bier in St. Patrick's Cathedral, and over 900 priests attended his funeral. The New York *Daily News* commented: "On Cardinal Cooke's final day, a line from Shakespeare seems uniquely appropriate: 'Nothing in his life became him like his leaving of it.' This was a man who showed us all how to pass from time to eternity with courage and grace."

Pope John Paul II at Yankee Stadium in 1979

Text of the last Pastoral Letter of Cardinal Cooke

This is Cardinal Cooke's letter on Respect Life Month, to be read at all Masses on the weekend, Oct. 8-9.

Cardinal's Residence
October 9, 1983

Dear Friends in Christ:

How often we speak of "the gift of life," God's "gift of life" to us, His sons and daughters. What a beautiful phrase! How filled with meaning it is! In the Book of Genesis, we read of the origin of this gift: "So God created man in His own image, in the image of God He created him; male and female He created them."

It is at times when life is threatened—such as times of serious illness—that the Lord gives us a special grace to appreciate "the gift of life" more deeply as an irreplaceable blessing which only God can give and which God must guide at every step. From the beginning of human life, from conception until death and at every moment in between, it is the Lord Our God Who gives us life, and we, who are His creatures, should cry out with joy and thanksgiving for this precious gift.

We are made in God's image and likeness, and this fact gives us a unique dimension to "the gift of life." We have even more reason to be grateful. It is tragic that in our time, concepts which are disastrous to the well-being of God's human family—abortion, euthanasia and infanticide—are falsely presented as useful and even respectable solutions to human, family and social problems. Human life is sometimes narrowly viewed in terms of being inconvenient or unwanted, unproductive or lacking arbitrarily imposed human criteria.

From the depths of my being, I urge you to reject this anti-life, anti-child, anti-human view of life and to oppose with all your strength the deadly technologies of life-destruction which daily result in the planned death of the innocent and the helpless. Together we must search for ways to demonstrate this conviction in our daily lives and in our public institutions. In doing so, we must never be discouraged or give up. Too much is at stake—"the gift of life" itself.

The "gift of life," God's special gift, is no less beautiful when it is accompanied by illness or weakness, hunger or poverty, mental or physical handicaps, loneliness or old age. Indeed, at these times, human life gains extra splendor as it requires our special care, concern and reverence. It is in and through the weakest of human vessels that the Lord continues to reveal the power of His love.

For the last ten years, I have served as Chairman of the Bishops' Committee for Pro-Life Activities in the United States. With God's help, I have tried to encourage and promote a Respect Life attitude throughout our nation. I have pleaded with you to pray and to be active in the many efforts for the enhancement and the protection of human life at every stage of existence.

In October, as we observe Respect Life Month, I call on you to rededicate your efforts for the sanctity of all human life and to work to counteract the contemporary threats to life. I urge you to increase and to strengthen the programs in our parishes and communities for the poor, the elderly, the handicapped, the rejected, the homeless, the suffering, the unwanted, the unborn. I ask you to focus attention again on the Pastoral Plan for Pro-Life Activities and on the three elements of education, pastoral care and public policy which are necessary if we are to work for and defend the most defenseless members of society.

At this grace-filled time of my life, as I experience suffering in union with Jesus, Our Lord and Redeemer, I offer gratitude to Almighty God for giving me the opportunity to continue my apostolate on behalf of life. I thank each one of you, my sisters and brothers in the Archdiocese of New York and throughout our nation, for what you have done and will do on behalf of human life. May we never yield to indifference or claim helplessness when innocent human life is threatened or when human rights are denied.

With you, I entrust our efforts to the care of Our Lady who, from the moment of her Immaculate Conception to the present, has been the refuge for the poorest and most forgotten among God's people. I assure you of a special share in the prayerful offerings of my sufferings to the Father, in union with Jesus and through the Spirit of Love Who is ours in abundance.

May God bless you always and give you His peace.

Devotedly yours in Christ,
Terence Cardinal Cooke
Archbishop of New York

# John Cardinal O'Connor

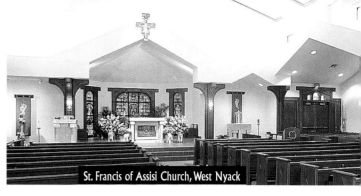

St. Francis of Assisi Church, West Nyack

John Cardinal O'Connor

The death of Cardinal Cooke, three weeks after the death of Humberto Cardinal Medeiros of Boston, gave Pope John Paul II the opportunity to fill two of the most important American sees. In both instances he picked men who reflected his own vision of the Church, Bernard Law for Boston, and John O'Connor for New York. The appointments occurred only months after Archbishop John Roach of St. Paul, the outgoing president of the National Conference of Catholic Bishops, had publicly denied rumors that the pope was unhappy with the leadership qualities of the American hierarchy. On the contrary, said Roach, "a new, important and positive chapter" had begun in the relationship between Rome and the American bishops.

Cardinal O'Connor and President Reagan

O'Connor was born in Philadelphia on January 15, 1920, and ordained a priest of that archdiocese on December 15, 1945. After several diocesan assignments, he had spent twenty-seven years as a navy chaplain, earning a doctorate in political science and rising to the position of chief of Navy chaplains with the rank of rear admiral. He was no stranger to New York, having lived in the city from 1979 to 1983 while serving as auxiliary bishop in the Military Ordinariate. Appointed bishop of Scranton, Pennsylvania, on May

10, 1983, he was promoted to New York only eight months later, on January 31, 1984. At sixty-four years of age, he was twenty-four years older than John Hughes when Hughes was appointed coadjutor bishop of New York, but O'Connor was to display an energy that even Hughes might have envied.

Much had changed in New York since the appointment Francis Spellman almost a half-century earlier, when the Monday morning newspapers still carried accounts of the previous Sunday's sermons in the principal churches. Religion had since been reduced to a peripheral role in public life by an aggressively secularistic culture, which promoted, among other objectives, a value-free acceptance of abortion and homosexuality. "In New York's liberal media, abortion is a religion," said William Reel, a veteran Catholic journalist. Spellman appeared in the pulpit of St. Patrick's Cathedral fewer than a dozen times during his twenty-eight years as arch-bishop, but he was able to wield enormous influence indirectly through the courtship paid to him by the city's power brokers. Robert Caro has described how, at the dedication of every new bridge and tunnel, riding in the first limousine with Robert Moses and "the mayor of the moment," was the diminutive figure of Cardinal Spellman, basking in the deference paid to him by New York's quintessential Power Broker.

By 1983, however, that cozy relationship of church and state had disappeared in New York with the erosion of Irish political power. Jimmy Breslin, the pugnacious

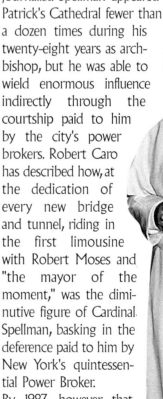

Pope John Paul II and Cardinal O'Connor

columnist for the tabloid New York *Daily News,* taunted the new archbishop as "Yesterday O'Connor" in the mistaken belief that he would try to resurrect Spellman's *modus operandi.* As O'Connor later admitted, he had indeed decided to move in a different direction from Cooke, but that decision did not mean an attempt to return to the halcyon days of Spellman. In the Secular City of the 1980s, there were no halcyon days for religious leaders, who had to fight for a hearing amid the clamor of many

St. Joseph's Church, Spring Valley

other competing voices in the public marketplace of ideas. John O'Connor signaled his awareness of the situation even before taking up his duties as the archbishop of New York. In a television interview a week before his installation, he drew an analogy between the legalization of abortion in the United States and the Holocaust in Nazi Germany. The *New York Times,* one of the prime arbiters of America's secular culture, pounced upon the interview to fire a warning shot across the bow of Admiral O'Connor's ship before it reached home port. In an editorial, the *Times* skewered O'Connor's incautious reference to Hitler's "Jewish problem" to imply that he was anti-Semitic and suggested sententiously that, "if he means to instruct the community at large, a change of tone would be welcome."

O'Connor's indignant rebuttal produced a half-hearted apology from the *Times,* under the guise of a clarification, and a grudging welcome to New York. Far more significant, however, was the letter that appeared a week later from Arthur J. Goldberg, former U.S. Supreme Court justice and chairman of the American Jewish Commission on the Holocaust. Goldberg recounted how O'Connor,

when chief of Navy chaplains, had arranged a visit to Dachau for the chief chaplains of the NATO forces. Any imputation of anti-Semitism, said Goldberg, "constitutes an unwarranted aspersion on Bishop O'Connor's total dedication to human rights and his total abhorrence of anti-Semitism in any form." John O'Connor was installed as the eighth archbishop of New York on March 19, 1984; a little over a year later, on May 25, 1985, he was made a Cardinal. During that first year, he established a style of leadership that he would continue throughout the rest of his episcopate. It resembled closely the leadership style of Pope John Paul II, with heavy emphasis on preaching and public appearances, the use of both the press and television, pastoral visits to parishes and institutions throughout the archdiocese, and the staging of special events such as an annual Mass for the disabled in St. Patrick's Cathedral and a youth rally at Yankee Stadium in the spring of 1985 that drew 40,000 people. At a gathering of 10,000 Cursillistas at the Marian Shrine in Haverstraw in August 1984, O'Connor delivered his first sermon in what he called "la lengua de Miguel Cervantes." A major theme in Cardinal O'Connor's public pronouncements was the threat to the sanctity of life posed by widespread acceptance of abortion and euthanasia. His fellow bishops recognized his contribution to the pro-life movement by electing him chairman of the Pro-Life Activities Committee of the NCCB in 1989. Another contentious public issue that tested O'Connor's mettle immediately upon his arrival in New York was the effort of the city's large and powerful gay

In a scene that would have been unthinkable before Vatican II, Cardinal O'Connor pays tribute to Rabbi Marc Tanenbaum during a service at the Park Avenue Synagogue on July 6, 1992

community to win public acceptance of their lifestyle. The new archbishop challenged a recently issued executive order of Mayor Edward Koch, regulating the hiring practices of private charitable institutions. The regulations were so broadly framed that O'Connor feared they would require Catholic child-caring institutions to hire even militant homosexual activists. "We would rather close our child-caring institutions than violate church teaching," said O'Connor. He won the court case on appeal, and the dispute did not damage his burgeoning friendship with Mayor Koch. "New York," said the Cardinal, "is the only place in the world where good friends sue one another."

The ongoing dispute with the gay community did not prevent the archdiocese from expanding its hospital and hospice program for victims of AIDS. "The health care institutions operated by the archdiocese were the very first to respond to the state's call for dedicated units to care for AIDs patients," said Governor Mario Cuomo in January 1990. "They were the first and they do the most. It's an inspiration to the community and it has shown leadership."

O'Connor also provided leadership on a number of other social issues, condemning racism, opposing Medicaid cuts in the state budget, offering support to labor unions, most notably the hospital workers' union, which represented some of the poorest paid workers in the city. In testimony before a Congressional subcommittee in 1985, he said that it was wrong to increase defense spending but not housing allocations. At the time of the immensely popular Persian Gulf War in 1991, the former admiral tried to temper the widespread euphoria by saying, "No war is good. Every war is at best the lesser of evils."

One area in which O'Connor achieved spectacular success was in establishing a close working relationship with the New York Jewish community. In February 1988 Ronald B. Sobel, the senior rabbi of Temple Emanu-El, said: "From the very moment that Cardinal John J. O'Connor was consecrated [sic] archbishop of New York, it was clear that the

Jewish people had found a new and powerful friend.... I know of no member of the American Catholic hierarchy who has been more consistently sensitive to the interests of the Jewish people." In 1992 the U.S. bishops signaled their agreement by choosing O'Connor to head the Catholic-Jewish Relations committee of the NCCB, and he was widely credited in the Jewish community with paving the way for the establishment of diplomatic relations between Israel and the Holy See.

Five years after O'Connor's arrival in New York, two perceptive observers of American Catholicism gave him high marks for his performance. Monsignor George Higgins, the heir of John A. Ryan and the Grand Old Man of Catholic social teaching in America, remarked that "the cardinal's record in support of social justice, if only because of his willingness to stand up and be counted on controversial issues, regardless of the cost, has relatively few parallels in the recent history of the American hierarchy." Monsignor John Tracy Ellis, for many years the dean of American Catholic historians and a close personal friend of O'Connor, characterized him as "a classic example of an oft-recurring type among modern churchmen who simultaneously portray a progressive attitude toward social questions with a conservative stand on theological matters." Although O'Connor disliked such political labels, Ellis placed him in good company, when he added: "One finds the combination evident in the lives of such men as Bishop von Ketteler of Mainz, Cardinal Manning of Westminster and Cardinal Gibbons of Baltimore."

On his fifth anniversary in New York, O'Connor wondered if he had devoted too much of his time to the media and regretted his inability to have more impact on the city's moral standards and social problems. However, that same year, a friendly non-Catholic critic, Joseph Berger, described the Cardinal as "a man of contradictions," but identified his deft use of the media as the source of his strength as a public figure. "Many local politicians believe that the Cardinal has already heightened the archdiocese's political

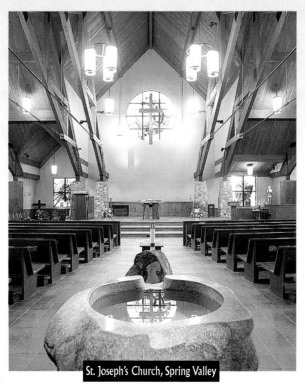

St. Joseph's Church, Spring Valley

St. Joseph's Church, Spring Valley

impact—its ability to move the city's bureaucracy on behalf of its extensive social programs and its power to get city policy makers to respect Catholic doctrine," said Berger. Moreover, he explained, "He has done this not so much through influential friends in business and politics, as Francis Cardinal Spellman did … but more through his assets as a communicator." Father Joseph Fitzpatrick, the Jesuit sociologist, also pointed out that O'Connor had to deal with issues that were far more controversial than those faced by any of his predecessors.

Eventually O'Connor himself seemed to recognize that he had spread himself too thin. In 1990 he discontinued the weekly press conferences after the 10:15 Sunday Mass in the cathedral, when, he said to an interviewer, the press corps "would come swooping in at the end and ask me about everything under the sun." "Well, what do I know about everything under the sun? But I would dutifully give them answers. And I said some dumb things." Nevertheless, in 1997, Father Thomas Reese, the Jesuit scholar and astute observer of the American hierarchy, described O'Connor as "the highest profile bishop in the country." "Part of that is because he is in New York, where all the media are located," explained Reese, "and part is due to his own personality and talents." The following year, when O'Connor tangled with Mayor Rudolph Giuliani over legislation to give domestic partners the same legal standing as married couples, his old nemesis, the *New York Times*, admitted that the Cardinal was "perhaps the one person in New York with a platform to rival that of the mayor."

# The Archdiocese on the Eve of the Millenium

Father John Grange, pastor of St. Jerome's Church, leads a procession down 138th Street in May 1992

After remaining fairly stagnant during the Cooke years, the Catholic population of the archdiocese increased from 1,839,000 to 2,347,000 between 1983 and 1998. In the archdiocese as a whole, Catholics constituted 45% of the total population. The growth in population was not reflected in sacramental practice, however, with the number of baptisms and marriages remaining virtually the same.

Original Church of St. Jerome, erected 1869, now the parish school

The complexity and variety of the archdiocese was astonishing, ranging from prosperous suburban villages to desperately poor inner city neighborhoods. In the wealthy Dutchess county hamlet of Millbrook, a major community concern was preserving access to 50,000 acres of private land for fox hunting. In the Bronx parish of Our Saviour, 58% of the families lived below the poverty line in the mid-1980s, and any foxes were likely to be of the two-legged kind. The pastor, Father Jesus Iriondo, C.R.L., said: "When I came to this country from the Basque region of Spain, I didn't expect to have to deal with basic problems of food, clothing and shelter." Poverty was not an exclusively urban phenomenon. In rural Sullivan county, an area of great natural beauty, the medium annual income of nearly one-fifth of the families was less than $7,500. "You have to get up here to see the poverty," said Cardinal O'Connor on a visit in the summer of 1991.

Sister Patricia Quinn, S.C., with Gina Rosales, a pupil at Sts. Peter and Paul School, in September 1989

Window of St. Francis of Assisi Church, New York City

The ethnic character of New York City neighborhoods was constantly in flux. St. Ann's parish in East Harlem, once a thriving Italian parish, by 1990 was 60% African American, 30% Puerto Rican and 10% Italian. In 1995, in the neighboring parish of Our Lady of Mount Carmel, the annual procession, made famous by Robert Orsi's book, *The Madonna of 115th Street*, was preceded by Masses in Italian, Spanish, French Creole and Latin. The Redemptorist parish of Most Holy Redeemer on the Lower East Side of Manhattan, once New York's German Catholic cathedral, where almost 10,000 people attended Mass every Sunday, was now home to 250 families, half English-speaking, half Spanish-speaking, who came, said the pastor, "from a great many nations."

Holy Name of Jesus parish on the Upper West Side of Manhattan nearly perished from urban blight in the 1960s, but experienced a renaissance as the neighborhood improved in the 1990s. "It was really like a phoenix," said the pastor. "It died and rose from the ashes," with 7,000 people attending seven Masses in three languages every Sunday. By contrast, when St. George's parish in upstate Jeffersonville celebrated its 150th anniversary in 1994, little had changed in a century and a half. The parish contained 370 families spread over 324 square miles. The same Franciscan friars who administered both parishes also staffed New York's most famous midtown business parish, St. Francis of Assisi, where they celebrated thirteen Masses everyday, heard confessions from 6:45 a.m. to 7:00 p.m., and fed the hungry at their noontime bread line.

An Irish Catholic who was raised in Highbridge and moved away in the 1950s was appalled at the changes that he noticed on periodic visits to his old neighborhood. "Apartment houses on Woodycrest Avenue that used to sing with the life of bustling families had become burnt-out tombs," he said. "The neighborhood library on Shakespeare Avenue was sealed over like a war-torn bunker. Even the great Church of the Sacred Heart, which still stands splendidly as a kind of mighty fortress, was locked shut after the morning Mass." The one beacon of hope that he found in the whole neighborhood was Sacred Heart School, where, he said, "the smiling, alert faces I saw that day ... belong to children who have had hope instilled in them."

The Church of New York remained the Immigrant Church, as it had been since the inception of the diocese in 1808. The single largest group of Catholic immigrants continued to be Hispanics. Immigrants from the Dominican Republic now outstripped those from Puerto Rico, and they were joined by growing numbers of immigrants from Mexico, Cuba, and the countries of Central and South America. Haitians too arrived in increasing numbers, and by the mid-1980s, at least 25,000 of them had settled in Rockland county.

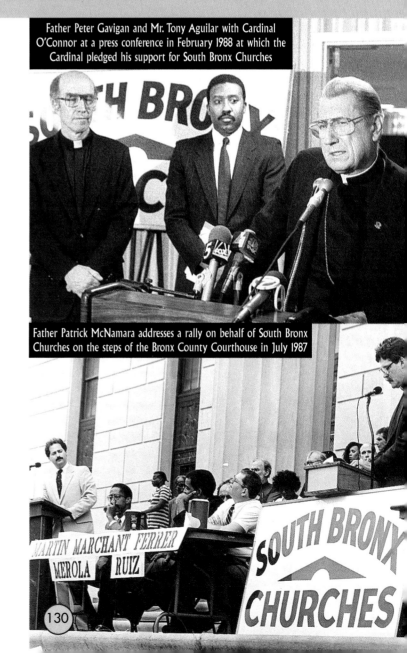

Father Peter Gavigan and Mr. Tony Aguilar with Cardinal O'Connor at a press conference in February 1988 at which the Cardinal pledged his support for South Bronx Churches

Father Patrick McNamara addresses a rally on behalf of South Bronx Churches on the steps of the Bronx County Courthouse in July 1987

A new phenomenon was the large number of Catholic immigrants from Asia, most notably Filipinos, Chinese, Vietnamese, and Koreans (who established the parish of St. John Nam in the Bronx in 1989). Albanians, Arabs, and Portuguese all added to the catholicity of the archdiocese, as did a sudden jump in the number of Irish immigrants, leading to the establishment of Project Irish Outreach in the north Bronx. Mass was celebrated every Sunday in at least twenty-two languages, with 135 of the 413 parishes providing Mass in Spanish.

Catholic education remained a high priority for the archdiocese. In the spring of 1985 Cardinal O'Connor told the Catholic school teachers that the schools would remain open "at whatever the sacrifice" necessary on the part of the archdiocese. The abrupt decline in enrollment that occurred during the 1970s stabilized with 108,355 students on the elementary and high school level. Minority students, many of them non-Catholic, made up almost half the enrollment. In 1986, 84% of the students in the Catholic elementary schools in Manhattan were African American, Hispanic or Asian. That same year, the U.S. Department of Education cited St. Ignatius school in Manhattan and Saints Peter and Paul school in the Bronx, both staffed by the Sisters of Charity, as two of the outstanding elementary schools in the nation.

The principal of Saint Peter and Paul school called it "an oasis in the desert." Bishop Henry Mansell, who had graduated from that school forty years earlier when the neighborhood was largely Irish, estimated in 1994 that it would cost the city an additional $1.2 billion dollars per year, if it had to educate all of the children in the parochial schools.

The archdiocesan school system, one of the largest school systems in the country, was a heavy financial burden. In 1965 there were 5,359 clerics and religious teaching in the Catholic schools of the archdiocese; by 1998, there were only 359 of them left. The transition to a largely lay teaching staff left the archdiocese in the unenviable position of trying to pay teachers a decent salary without raising the tuition beyond the reach of most parents. The decline in the numbers of diocesan clergy to 588 active priests also made it increasingly difficult to staff parishes, although the number of permanent deacons, the first of whom were ordained in 1973, grew to 310. Two new religious communities were founded, the Sisters of Life and the Franciscan Friars of the Renewal.

The Catholic Church remained a major provider of social services with 17 hospitals, 3 health care centers, 17 homes for the aged, and 19 child-caring institutions. Catholic hospitals were leaders in

The new William D. Walsh Family Library at the Rose Hill campus of Fordham University

providing care for AIDS patients as was the Gift of Love, a hospice founded by Mother Teresa's Missionaries of Charity in Greenwich Village. In addition, the archdiocese operated 129 different social agencies. No one appreciated their contribution to the city more than Mayor Koch, who said, "They provided the best social services that were available."

The Church's presence was also evident in the construction and renovation of affordable housing in Highbridge, East Harlem, the Lower East Side of Manhattan and other devastated neighborhoods. One of the most promising developments was the formation in 1987 of South Bronx Churches, a nonpartisan, ecumenical organization spearheaded by the priests of the South Bronx. Explaining the purpose of the organization, Father Peter Gavigan said: "We have to help the people become agents of change." At a rally and "accountability session" which drew 1,000 people to the steps of the Bronx County Courthouse that year, Rudolph Giuliani, then the U.S. Attorney for the southern district of New York, told the crowd: "This gathering is the most appropriate way I know to celebrate 200 years of the Constitution. You are making that promise of 'We the People' a reality." Cardinal O'Connor called it "one of the most important and exciting things that has happened in New York" and pledged his unconditional support.

# The Pope and the Millenium

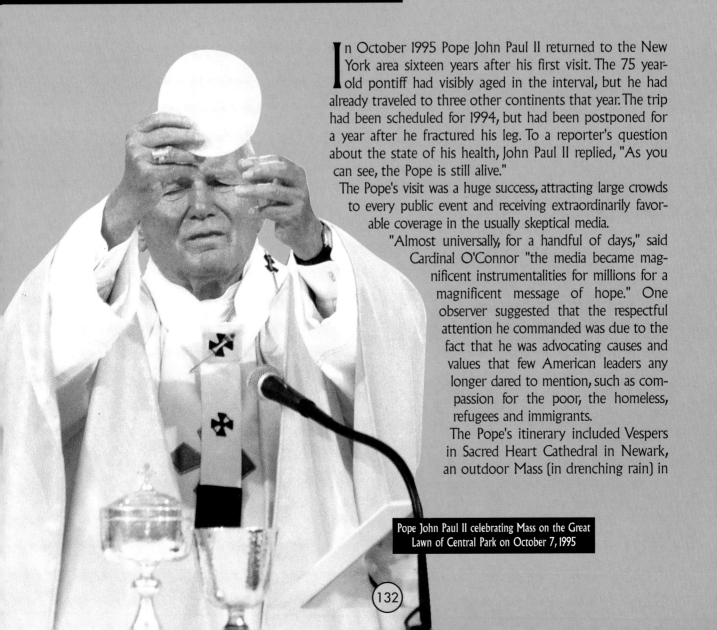

In October 1995 Pope John Paul II returned to the New York area sixteen years after his first visit. The 75 year-old pontiff had visibly aged in the interval, but he had already traveled to three other continents that year. The trip had been scheduled for 1994, but had been postponed for a year after he fractured his leg. To a reporter's question about the state of his health, John Paul II replied, "As you can see, the Pope is still alive."

The Pope's visit was a huge success, attracting large crowds to every public event and receiving extraordinarily favorable coverage in the usually skeptical media.

"Almost universally, for a handful of days," said Cardinal O'Connor "the media became magnificent instrumentalities for millions for a magnificent message of hope." One observer suggested that the respectful attention he commanded was due to the fact that he was advocating causes and values that few American leaders any longer dared to mention, such as compassion for the poor, the homeless, refugees and immigrants.

The Pope's itinerary included Vespers in Sacred Heart Cathedral in Newark, an outdoor Mass (in drenching rain) in

Pope John Paul II celebrating Mass on the Great Lawn of Central Park on October 7, 1995

132

Pope John Paul II arriving at St Patrick's Cathedral for a rosary service

Giants Stadium, an address to the General Assembly of the United Nations, another outdoor Mass in Aqueduct Race Track, and a visit to St. Joseph's Seminary, Dunwoodie. For New Yorkers, however, the highlight of the Pope's visit, was a Mass on October 7 on the Great Lawn in Central Park before 125,000 people, many of whom had arrived in the pre-dawn darkness because of stringent security procedures.

Speaking alternately in Spanish and English at the Central Park Mass, the Pope made an impassioned plea for the sanctity of life and social justice. "You are called to respect and defend the mystery of life always and everywhere," the Pope said, "including the lives of unborn babies." He also called upon his listeners to "stand up" for the life of the aged and handicapped, the poor, homeless, and hungry, for "those who are alone or are ill, for example those suffering from AIDS."

Cardinal O'Connor displays the chalice that Pope John Paul II presented to St. Joseph's Seminary on the occasion of his visit

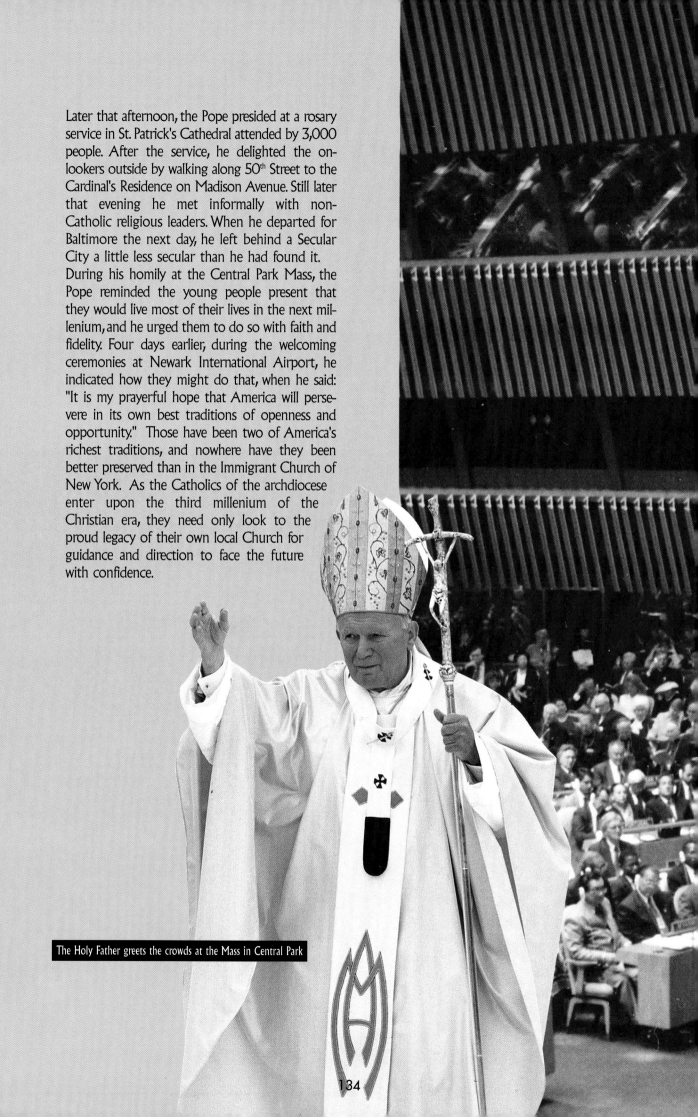

Later that afternoon, the Pope presided at a rosary service in St. Patrick's Cathedral attended by 3,000 people. After the service, he delighted the onlookers outside by walking along 50th Street to the Cardinal's Residence on Madison Avenue. Still later that evening he met informally with non-Catholic religious leaders. When he departed for Baltimore the next day, he left behind a Secular City a little less secular than he had found it.

During his homily at the Central Park Mass, the Pope reminded the young people present that they would live most of their lives in the next millenium, and he urged them to do so with faith and fidelity. Four days earlier, during the welcoming ceremonies at Newark International Airport, he indicated how they might do that, when he said: "It is my prayerful hope that America will persevere in its own best traditions of openness and opportunity." Those have been two of America's richest traditions, and nowhere have they been better preserved than in the Immigrant Church of New York. As the Catholics of the archdiocese enter upon the third millenium of the Christian era, they need only look to the proud legacy of their own local Church for guidance and direction to face the future with confidence.

The Holy Father greets the crowds at the Mass in Central Park

134

The Holy Father addresses the General
Assembly of the United Nations

Pope John Paul II at the Central Park Mass beneath the banner depicting the ethnic diversity of New York's Immigrant Church

# BIBLIOGRAPHY

BIBLIOGRAPHY

■ John Tracy Ellis,
*American Catholicism, 2nd edn.*
(Chicago, 1969).

■ Florence D. Cohalan,
*A Popular History of the Archdiocese of New York*
(Yonkers, 1983).

■ Jay P. Dolan,
*The Immigrant Church:*
*New York's Irish and German Catholics, 1815–1865*
(Baltimore, 1975).

■ John Talbot Smith,
*History of the Church in New York*
(New York and Boston, 1905), 2 vols

■ Francis X. Curran, S.J.,
*The Return of the Jesuits*
(Chicago, 1966).

■ Richard Shaw,
*Dagger John, The Unquiet Life and Times of Archbishop John Hughes of New York*
(New York, 1977).

■ Richard Shaw,
*John Dubois: Founding Father*
(Yonkers, 1983).

■ John R. G. Hassard,
*Life of the Most Reverend John Hughes*
(New York, 1866).

■ Stephen DiGiovanni,
*Archbishop Corrigan and the Italian Immigrants*
(Huntington, IN, 1994).

■ Robert Emmet Curran, S.J.,
*Michael Augustine Corrigan and the Shaping of Conservative Catholicism in America (1878–1902)*
(New York, 1978).

■ Marvin R. O'Connell,
*Archbishop John Ireland and the American Catholic Church*
(St. Paul, 1988).

■ Ella M.E. Flick,
*Chaplain Duffy of the Sixty–Ninth Regiment, New York.*
Philadelphia, 1935.

■ Ana Maria Diaz-Stevens,
*Oxcart Catholicism on Fifth Avenue: The Impact of the Puerto Rican Migration upon the Archdiocese of New York.* Notre Dame, 1993.

■ Gerald P. Fogarty, S.J.,
*"Francis J. Spellman, American and Roman," in Fogarty, ed., Patterns of Episcopal Leadership.* New York, 1989.

■ Robert I. Gannon, S.J.,
*The Cardinal Spellman Story.* New York, 1962.

■ Benedict J. Groeschel, C.F.R., and Terrence L. Weber,
*Thy Will Be Done: A Spiritual Portrait of Terence Cardinal Cooke.* Staten Island, N.Y., 1990.

■ Nat Hentoff,
*John Cardinal O'Connor: At the Storm Center of a Changing Catholic Church.* New York, 1988.

■ Jill Jonnes,
*We're Still Here: The Rise, Fall and Resurrection of the South Bronx.* Boston and New York, 1986.

■ John Cardinal O'Connor and Edward Koch,
*His Eminence and Hizzoner.* New York, 1989.

■ Robert Orsi,
*The Madonna of 115th Street: Faith and Community in Italian Harlem, 1880–1950.* New Haven, 1985.

■ Thomas J. Shelley,
*Dunwoodie: The History of St. Joseph's Seminary.*
Westminster, MD, 1992

Publisher

ÉDITIONS
DU SIGNE

Éditions du Signe
BP 94 - 67038 Strasbourg Cedex 2
Tél 03 88 78 91 91 - Fax 03 88 78 91 99
Layout
Carré Blanc
Photos
Yvon Meyer
Chris Sheridan
© Éditions du Signe 1999 - All rights reserved
ISBN 2-87718-819-1
Printed in Italy by Albagraf, Roma